THANK GOD

THANK GOD

Becoming More Grateful to the Greatest of Givers

Reuben Bredenhof

Reformation Heritage Books
Grand Rapids, Michigan

Thank God
© 2023 by Reuben Bredenhof

Reformation Heritage Books
3070 29th St. SE
Grand Rapids, MI 49512
616-977-0889
orders@heritagebooks.org
www.heritagebooks.org

Unless otherwise indicated, Scripture quotations taken from the New King James Version®. Copyright © 1982 by Thomas Nelson. Used by permission. All rights reserved.

Scripture quotations marked ESV are from The Holy Bible, English Standard Version® (ESV®), copyright © 2001 by Crossway, a publishing ministry of Good News Publishers. Used by permission. All rights reserved.

Scripture quotations marked NIV are from THE HOLY BIBLE, NEW INTERNATIONAL VERSION®, NIV® Copyright © 1973, 1978, 1984, 2011 by Biblica, Inc.® Used by permission. All rights reserved worldwide.

All italics in Scripture quotations have been added by the author.

Printed in the United States of America
23 24 25 26 27 28/10 9 8 7 6 5 4 3 2 1

Library of Congress Cataloging-in-Publication Data

Names: Bredenhof, Reuben, author.
Title: Thank God : becoming more grateful to the greatest of givers / Reuben Bredenhof.
Description: Grand Rapids, Michigan : Reformation Heritage Books, 2023. | Includes bibliographical references and index.
Identifiers: LCCN 2022054668 (print) | LCCN 2022054669 (ebook) | ISBN 9781601789945 (paperback) | ISBN 9781601789952 (epub)
Subjects: LCSH: Gratitude—Religious aspects—Christianity.
Classification: LCC BV4647.G8 B74 2023 (print) | LCC BV4647.G8 (ebook) | DDC 241/.4—dc23/eng/20230215
LC record available at https://lccn.loc.gov/2022054668
LC ebook record available at https://lccn.loc.gov/2022054669

For additional Reformed literature, request a free book list from Reformation Heritage Books at the above regular or email address.

DEDICATION

To the elders and deacons
of the Free Reformed Church
of Mount Nasura, Western Australia,
with my gratitude.

Contents

Preface

At the beginning of September 2020, I was looking forward to a three-month sabbatical. Near the top of the long list of things to do while enjoying a break from my duties as a pastor was to write a book about gratitude. Because it was an idea that I had mulled over for years, I was thankful for the opportunity to have an extended period to tackle this project.

Another activity a little further down my sabbatical to-do list was to run a half-marathon. I thought that this was not an unrealistic goal, considering that I have been running regularly for more than fifteen years. Leading up to the 21.1-kilometer race, I intensified my training and lengthened my daily runs. I entertained no doubt that I would be able to complete it. I wouldn't set any records but would most certainly collect my finisher's medal at the finish line.

It was a beautiful, sunny Saturday early that September when I gathered with about two hundred other runners along the scenic Swan River in Perth, Western Australia, to run my half-marathon. With race shirts donned, shoes tied, running gels ready, and sport watches set to go, we excitedly began our event.

And I think that the race went really well for me—until the last three hundred meters or so. I remember nothing of what happened in those minutes. But apparently, I started to sway badly on my feet and to lose all forward momentum. Being so close to the end of the race, I behaved like I was determined to reach the finish line. But it was clear that I could not. Bystanders helped to lower me safely to the ground, where I received care while we waited for the ambulance to arrive.

Finally returning to my senses (at least partially) on a stretcher in the back of the ambulance, my first thoughts were dominated by immense disappointment: *I can't believe this. I did not complete the race.* So close, yet so far. Together with that painful regret there was a concern for my wife and daughters. I knew they would be distressed, seeing me passed out on the ground and then loaded into the ambulance.

And then there were feelings of embarrassment, uncertainty, and anxiety. In those moments a whole cocktail of unpleasant emotions was rapidly coursing through me. I am supposed to be fit and strong, and I had collapsed in a heap on the grass. I like to think of myself as somewhat intelligent, but when the nurse asked, I wasn't even sure what year it was or how to spell my surname. My plan for that sunny Saturday certainly had not included an ambulance ride, a hospital admission, and a whole range of blood tests, heart checks, and IV drips. But there I was, and I hated it.

God is good and faithful, so He did not leave me in that low and miserable place. My outlook—which was pretty bleak for an hour or two—was soon enlightened by the unfailing presence of the Holy Spirit. And I noticed that, remarkably, among His other graces on that day and the following days, He gave me the gift of gratitude.

I was thankful to God for the willing help of numerous bystanders, among whom were a few with medical training.

I was thankful for the professional care of the paramedics—so calm, so competent.

I was thankful for my wife, Rebecca, who stood by me, prayed with me, and made sure I knew that I was loved.

I was thankful to live in a country where I had free access to excellent health care.

I was thankful for my four daughters, who quickly sent me get-well notes and things to make my time in the hospital more cheerful.

I was thankful for my church community, who immediately reached out with loving concern and who held me up in prayer.

I was thankful for God's Word, especially for the powerful prayers of the Psalms that I could remember in those first hours when I didn't have a Bible to read.

I was thankful for the good friends who gladly stepped in to make a difficult day a bit easier for our family.

I was thankful for the gift of prayer, for being able to speak with God and to know that He is near, always.

I was thankful for good health, how despite this incident, God has blessed me with physical strength and vitality.

I was thankful for running, an activity that I still love—just at shorter distances!

I was thankful for how God was graciously teaching me lessons about humility and dependence and trust.

I was thankful for the assurance that God's love never depends on my condition, status, or accomplishments, but that it is free and enduring for Jesus's sake.

I was thankful for a few quiet days in the hospital, time to take a deep breath, to read, to reflect, and to pray.

To God, my faithful Father, I was thankful for so much.

So this was how I began my sabbatical—just five days in, actually—shortly before I started working on this book. I began it with a crash course in what it means to be grateful.

I am aware that this half-marathon hardship can be dismissed as a "first-world problem." That is a term sometimes used to disparage the so-called adversities endured by wealthy and privileged people (like myself). It's a first-world problem when we complain about things like inattentive service at all-inclusive vacation resorts, over-done croissants at cafés, and disappointing returns on our investment portfolios. When people of our socioeconomic class gripe about the petty disturbances and frustrations that afflict our otherwise comfortable and tidy lives, it is hard to feel sympathetic. A half-marathon DNF (did not finish) will never be counted among life's great trials. Even so, for me and my family, that weekend's experience was a genuine difficulty. It was unsettling and humbling, and God used it to gently teach and shape me.

And so after a few days in the hospital for observation, I was thankful that I could go home. It was time to tackle my sabbatical to-do list and to get going on that gratitude book. On these pages I hope to instill in every reader a deeper and truer gratitude to our triune God, the God of all grace.

Acknowledgments

Where else can I begin a book about gratitude but with many thanks?

First, I want to express my great appreciation to the council of the Free Reformed Church of Mount Nasura, Western Australia. I was privileged to serve as the pastor of this congregation for seven and a half years. On the occasion of my fifteenth year in the pastoral ministry, the elders and deacons generously granted me a three-month sabbatical. The brothers gave me this time away from regular duties so that I could rest and recharge. They were careful to emphasize that there was absolutely no pressure to "produce" something during this time, but they of course knew that I wanted to. Indeed, for a long time I have hoped to write about gratitude, and the sabbatical presented an auspicious opportunity. This project would not have been completed without the care, encouragement, and prayers of the elders and deacons of the Mount Nasura council. So thank you, brothers! It was a privilege and a joy to work alongside you for the time that God gave us. I pray that God will use this book to bless His people in Australia and far beyond.

Second, I heartily thank the congregation of Mount Nasura. It was a delight to serve among you and to share fellowship throughout the time of our family's sojourn in Western Australia. When I was on my sabbatical and later was trying to nudge this project toward the finish line, the congregation blessed me with their interest and support. Thank you, brothers and sisters!

Third, I would be remiss if I did not acknowledge the countless people who answered my question, "What are you thankful for?" Many of these good folks were from my own congregation in Mount Nasura but also from nearby churches and even farther afield, in other time zones and distant countries. I thank all my conversation partners for their willingness to share their thoughts and ideas about gratitude. Above all, it was a blessing to hear their personal testimonies to God's goodness and faithfulness. For me, hearing people's unscripted and heartfelt answers to this question was inspiring and encouraging. Their words really gave color and depth to much of what you will find on the following pages.

Fourth, there is once again a long list of people who read various drafts and iterations of this book and who provided me with excellent feedback. I thank my sister in the Lord, Renee Mulder, who carefully read every page and found many typos and grammatical infelicities. I thank Elton Swarts, my brother and fellow elder, for his warm encouragement and wise comments. My colleague Rev. Art van Delden read through the whole book too and offered his pastoral perspective on some of the key ideas, particularly in relation to our thankfulness to God during times of suffering. I thank my friend Dr. Derek Swarts for sitting down with me over a cup of coffee (tea, in his case) on various occasions to chat about the book and to make helpful suggestions.

By now, our daughters are used to the routine of reading through drafts of my books and dropping their comments throughout. Besides being sharp-eyed editors, they were also good conversation partners about this topic. I think that it has been a blessing to make this book into another "family project." Thank you, Abigail, Kyra, Sasha, and Tori! And of course, I thank my wife, Rebecca, for everything that she contributed to *Thank God*. She can surely attest to how many years I talked about writing this book. And once I finally got started on it, she was more than willing to help me with her careful proofreading and through much discussion about its contents. We have been married for more than twenty years, and in these years with Rebecca at my side, I have been so blessed to learn how true are the words of Proverbs 18:22: "He who finds a wife finds a good thing, and obtains favor from the LORD." I thank God often for the gift of Rebecca.

Fifth, I am grateful to work together with Reformation Heritage Books on another project. I thank Dr. Jay Collier for his editorial guidance, Annette Gysen for her excellent copyediting, and David Woollin for his support.

Finally, something that can never be said often enough: thanks be to God! I am grateful that God gave me the desire, energy, insight, and opportunity to work on this book. Much more than this, I thank God for His unfailing love and steadfast mercy in adopting me as His child and uniting me to Christ my Savior. There is no greater gift. I gratefully acknowledge that everything I have, I have received. To God alone be all the glory!

CHAPTER 1

What Do You Have That You Did Not Receive?

What do you have that you did not receive? This question makes a person stop and think. Read the question again: *What do you have that you did not receive?* The question invites—even demands—our reflection. When I look at everything I have, how much of it has been given to me by another, and for how much of it do I have myself to thank?

Taking Inventory

This question requires our reflection for at least two reasons. First, it is good for us to think about what we actually have.

Some years ago, my wife and I and our four daughters migrated to Australia after I accepted a pastoral position at a church near Perth, Western Australia. Part of the prolonged and complicated process of this continental shift involved taking a complete inventory of the contents of our house in London, Canada. All the objects that would be loaded into the big shipping container had to be itemized and counted. This was so that the vigilant people at the Australian border control could know exactly what we were bringing into the country.

If you have ever done a similar inventory of your home, then you know that it involves page after page of tedious spreadsheet notations. We had to enumerate everything—from our girls' cherished collection of Polly Pockets, to the seven mixing bowls from the kitchen, to the rusty shovel and sledgehammer in the garden shed. After weeks of taking inventory and then two exhausting days watching the moving company load it all into a forty-foot sea container, it became clear to us just how much stuff we have!

Tightly packed into the container were only our material possessions, of course—the things that we perhaps value the least of all. What else do we have? Things impracticable to quantify or describe, to tally or document. For instance, among the six members of our family we have a vast repository of memories, both individual and collective: Bible songs we love to belt out together and memories of spring-break vacations in Myrtle Beach, school successes, joyous family celebrations of birthdays and Christmases, and a few sad yet grace-filled days. There are countless more recollections of lives lived under the Father's care, memories impossible to comprehensively document but unthinkable to disregard. We also have the rich blessings of relationships: husband and wife, mother and daughter, daughter and grandfather, cousin and cousin, friends, brothers and sisters in Christ, and many more. What is more, each of us individually has different talents, lessons that we've learned, and plans we've made. We have so much.

And then we have God. Not that we can hold onto Him like our favorite book, but in a very real sense, God is ours and we are His. Through this relationship of love comes an entire universe of blessing: adoption, forgiveness, renewal, wisdom, fellowship, and everlasting life. A full inventory of God's gifts of salvation would be impossible. It's kind of like what John said at the conclusion of his account of Jesus's ministry, "And there are also many other things that Jesus did, which if they were written one by one, I suppose that even the world itself could not contain the books that would be written" (John 21:25).

What do you have? No child of God could ever give a comprehensive account in answer to this important question. I suppose that even all the Excel spreadsheets in the world would be inadequate to record the riches of what redeemed sinners have received. And yet we give thanks.

On the Receiving End

What do you have? That is the first part of the question. Now for the second part: What do you have *that you did not receive?*

I could answer that question superficially. I could run my eye over our home inventory and say that with my own hard-earned money I purchased almost every single one of those many books, our television, the bed linens, and nearly everything else too. Only the coffee table was a gift, some of the board games, and a few of the older and chunkier wine glasses. As for the memories that I have, they are my own, of course—it was I who experienced all those moments. Also mine are a good number of the aforementioned relationships I have chosen to enter and I make the ongoing effort to maintain. And as for my competency in expository preaching or my ability to shoot a basketball, these are skills I have slowly developed through diligent study and regular practice. I could go on, asserting that these and many more such things have not been *given* to me outright. After all, I have been personally involved in choosing and acquiring and sustaining them. What's mine is mine!

But the question is not meant to be considered superficially. It should not be answered with the self-made individual's quick nod to purchases transacted and personal choices made. A more profound question would be about the source of all things in your life. Indeed, what is the origin of your life itself? What do you have that you did not receive?

The first person to ask this question was the apostle Paul in a letter he wrote to the Corinthians. He was their father in the faith and part-time pastor. And he wanted these believers to think carefully about how full they were in Christ, how rich, how privileged. He desired that they ponder the true source of all these blessings: "What do you have that you did not receive?" (1 Cor. 4:7).

In posing this searching question to the Corinthians, Paul is subtly rebuking them. When they surveyed all their advantages and gains and celebrated their ability to speak in tongues and heal sickness, it is as if Paul asks them, "Tell me, did you earn any of it? Is any of this a credit to your own goodness or a result of your own effort or the product of your own wisdom?" And like every good rhetorical question, this one prompts people to see the obvious. Absolutely everything the Corinthians possessed was given to them. Absolutely everything that *I* have is a gift.

Over the ages, many Christians have meditated on Paul's question. Its probing query reveals the heart of what it means to be a human being, and particularly what it means to be a child of God, redeemed by His grace in Christ. This question humbles the proud, enlightens the ignorant, and refocuses the preoccupied.

Paul's quiet rebuke is made more unequivocal with his follow-up question in the second half of the verse: "Now if you did indeed receive it, why do you boast as if you had not received it?" The Corinthians were, in fact, bragging about their spiritual gifts and lauding their charismatic leaders. They acted as if it was all to their credit. But those who are the recipients of another person's generosity really have nothing to brag about. If we enjoy an advantaged position, special privileges, and notable gifts, it is all through the Father's benevolence. Then we dare not boast in our status or achievements, but we ought to be grateful. Nor do we dare to be selfish by hoarding or squandering what has been entrusted to our care, but we ought to be giving.

The linked questions of 1 Corinthians 4:7 prompt me to review my life and all that is in it. I look at not just the material things that can be tidily detailed on a spreadsheet, but the relational gifts, the communal, the emotional and spiritual. And I need to see that everything I have and everything I am are given. What do I have that I did not receive? Absolutely nothing! God's gifts have abounded from the moment when I was conceived and even long before, as He prepared and accomplished my salvation through Christ. I have always been on the receiving end. And this leaves just one response: gratitude.

Give Thanks

Somehow, we all know that when we have been given a special something, gratitude is the right attitude. From a very early time in every child's life, parents seek to include words of thanks on his or her list of key vocabulary phrases. Almost intuitively, we understand that saying "thank you" to other people is polite, is socially appropriate—that it is just *right*.

What is true for our interactions with other people is also true for our relationship with God: it is only right that we thank Him. For everything that God has graciously given and for all God is, we ought to acknowledge Him with thanksgiving. Such gratitude is an essential part of remembering what is true about us and what is true about God. We need to be ever mindful that we are wholly undeserving and that God is richly generous.

Just like parents will rightly expect their children to be grateful, so God expects this from us, those He made in His own image. Thanksgiving is commanded repeatedly in the Scriptures, such as in 1 Thessalonians 5:18: "In everything give thanks" (see also Ps. 107:1; Eph. 5:20). Yes, it is divinely commanded as well as being ethically expected. Yet in coming chapters we'll see that thanksgiving should also be the instinctive response of a person who has been redeemed and renewed through Christ. We come to delight in gratitude, and we love to show it to the Giver.

Indeed, a truly grateful response to God's benevolence is more than an emotion, more than just a passing feeling of appreciation. As far as feelings go, perhaps it is easy or natural for anyone to have a sentiment that borders on thankfulness. After a hearty meal or a productive day at work, we sit back and say, "Boy, I sure am thankful! I have definitely been blessed." It's an appropriate feeling. But where do we channel our surge of thankfulness? Where does the response travel from our grateful heart? Because of the nature of our hearts, the feeling quickly dissipates, and the emotion subsides. Soon the good things that have been granted are soon taken for granted.

For this reason, I want to develop and promote the God-given ability to give thanks in all circumstances. In doing this, I recognize that by nature we're ungrateful and discontented people. Growth in gratitude requires that we put to death our innate sense of entitlement and give up our habitual dissatisfaction. Instead, we aim to increase in our loving response to God.

In exploring gratitude together, we recognize that we are not able to repay God for all His goodness toward us. This is what the psalmist asks in Psalm 116 as he recounts how God mercifully delivered him from death: "What shall I render to the LORD for all His benefits toward me?" (v. 12). What can I ever give to the One who has given so much? Of course, I cannot reimburse Him. But I *can* praise Him. Such is the awe-filled response of a person who has been given everything. Even if our humble thankfulness to God will never be proportionate to His immense goodness toward us, we want to say it and show it.

A Resurgent Thanksgiving

There is no doubt that gratitude has become a popular topic in recent years. A quick foray into social media reveals that gratitude continues to be the object of many pretty memes. A discerning shopper can fill her home with daily reminders of the need for gratitude, from the "Give Thanks" exhortation on her coffee mug to the "Grateful" artwork on the living room wall.

Thankfulness has been the subject of many best-selling self-help books in the last couple of decades. There has also been a profusion of scientific research into the psychology of gratitude. Numerous experts have touted the importance of thankfulness for leading a happy and healthy life. For instance, studies have demonstrated that people who regularly express thankfulness enjoy its results through an alleviation of stress: "When you are grateful, all the signposts of stress, like anger, anxiety and worry, diminish."[1] Similarly, making a commitment to gratitude is said to enrich interpersonal love, encourage mental and physical well-being, improve patterns of sleep, and even increase life expectancy.

To promote thankfulness, psychologists recommend mindfulness practices like the daily gratitude inventory. Taking such an inventory requires us to pause, review, relish, and respond.[2] Individuals

---

1. Janice Kaplan, *The Gratitude Diaries* (London: Yellow Kite Books, 2015), 194.
2. Charles M. Shelton, *The Gratitude Factor: Enhancing Your Life through Grateful Living* (Mahwah, N.J.: HiddenSpring, 2010), 23.

may cultivate a more grateful spirit by pausing amid the daily busyness, reviewing their various gifts, relishing the value and worth of these gifts, and then responding with appreciation. The popularity of gratitude journals—in which you're meant to record a few of the good things that you received and appreciated every day—reflects the same impulse: *I want to be a thankful person.*

In some respects, the broad recognition of the importance of gratitude is remarkable. When we see in Scripture how fundamental thankfulness should be in the life of a believer who fears God, it is striking to find the same emphasis among those who don't know God through Christ. And there are useful insights to be gained through their reflections and mindfulness exercises.

But God-less gratitude is empty gratitude. Vague notions of "feeling good for the good things you have" is not at all like the gratitude a Christian learns to practice. In an approach that often has little place for God, secular gratitude becomes a means for a person to enhance his or her own life and is not a response to the Giver. The numerous personal benefits of thankfulness are trumpeted so that gratitude actually becomes a path to personal happiness. Through being a more grateful person, I will be able to improve my own life and outlook. Through my thankfulness for various good gifts, I will be able to attract more good gifts.

Ironically—and grievously—this self-focused gratitude is an inversion of what true gratitude is meant to be: a worshipful response to the One who has shown us His free and endless generosity. In answer to the question "What does it mean to repay in life?" Os Guinness observes, "By its very character, the modern world answers: You owe nothing. By its very character, the Christian gospel answers: You owe everything."[3]

A God-Less Gratitude

The hollowness of God-less gratitude is displayed every year in

---

3. Os Guinness, *The Call*, rev. and expanded 20th anniversary ed. (Nashville, Tenn.: Thomas Nelson, 2018), 259.

countries that observe Thanksgiving Day as an official holiday. If you reflect for a moment, you see that this is a strange festival for a largely nonbelieving society to celebrate. After all, thankfulness is something that you express *to* someone else. If my wife gives me a birthday gift of new socks and a bookstore gift card, I tell her that I am thankful, and I try to show her my gratitude. Yet when a nonbeliever celebrates Thanksgiving Day, who is being thanked?

It is good to remember that Thanksgiving Day was not always so objectless. In Canada, for instance, a day was devoted to thanksgiving from an early time in the nation's history. The practice was reconfirmed in 1957 when Parliament proclaimed the second Monday of October to be "A Day of General Thanksgiving to Almighty God for the bountiful harvest with which Canada has been blessed." This is gratitude with an object, albeit generically framed: Almighty God who grants blessing.

Similarly, in the United States, Abraham Lincoln issued the first presidential thanksgiving proclamation in October 1863:

> The year that is drawing towards its close has been filled with the blessings of fruitful fields and healthful skies. To these bounties, which are so constantly enjoyed that we are prone to forget the source from which they come, others have been added, which are of so extraordinary a nature, that they cannot fail to penetrate and soften even the heart which is habitually insensible to the ever watchful providence of Almighty God.... No human counsel hath devised nor hath any mortal hand worked out these great things. They are the gracious gifts of the Most High God, who, while dealing with us in anger for our sins, hath nevertheless remembered mercy. It has seemed to me fit and proper that they should be solemnly, reverently and gratefully acknowledged as with one heart and one voice by the whole American People.[4]

---

4. "Proclamation of Thanksgiving," in *Collected Works of Abraham Lincoln*, ed. Roy P. Basler et al. (New Brunswick, N.J.: Rutgers University Press, 1953–1955), https://www.abrahamlincolnonline.org/lincoln/speeches/thanks.htm.

Whatever governments have declared, psychologists advocated, or etiquette experts advised, thanksgiving has always been the holy response of God's people. Not just for one day per year but our whole lives long, God desires that His children be filled with gratitude: "And whatever you do in word or deed, do all in the name of the Lord Jesus, *giving thanks to God the Father through Him*" (Col. 3:17).

The Joyful Duty of Thanksgiving

So what is thankfulness? It is the grateful response in the heart and life of a redeemed sinner to the loving works of the triune God. Thankful people acknowledge that God has acted graciously toward them, and they express appreciation to God for His many benefits and blessings.

On the coming pages, I will alternate my use of *gratitude* and *thankfulness*. But if I were pressed to distinguish between them, I would describe *gratitude* in terms of the inward response of the spirit to God. *Thankfulness/thanksgiving* is the expression of this gratitude to God for mercies received.[5]

I have already said that God commands our thanksgiving. Because we are the recipients of God's good gifts, gratitude is nothing less than our holy obligation. The Scriptures are replete with God's demand that His redeemed people present Him with their thanksgiving.[6] As the church father Ambrose said many centuries ago, "No duty is more urgent than that of returning thanks."[7]

But what God sets forth as a sacred duty actually becomes our true delight. When we know more of God's greatness and recognize the magnitude of His love in Christ, the Holy Spirit moves us to respond with true thanksgiving. John Baillie writes, "A true Christian is a man who never for a moment forgets what God has done for him in Christ and whose whole comportment and whose activity

---

5. E. M. Bounds helpfully describes *thanksgiving*: "It is giving something to God in words that we feel at heart for blessings received." From "Essentials of Prayer," in *E. M. Bounds on Prayer* (New Kensington, Pa.: Whitaker House, 1997), 306.
6. See, e.g., Eph. 5:20; Phil. 4:6; Col. 2:7; 3:15, 17; 4:2.
7. Ambrose, *On the Death of Satyrus*, 1:44

have their root in the sentiment of gratitude."[8] Such thanksgiving
is not just the spontaneous response to gifts received. Rather, gratitude becomes the worshipful atmosphere in which a Christian lives.
Thankfulness saturates our thoughts, shapes our words, and directs
our habits.

It is through the regular practice of gratitude that we become
rightly oriented toward God. Daily we cherish how much He has
given, and we reflect on how it is all a gift of His grace. Henri Nouwen
describes this as a discipline for the believer's life, a holy perspective
that is learned and then allowed to shape everything that he or she
does: "The discipline of gratitude is the explicit effort to acknowledge that all I am and have is given to me as a gift of love, a gift to be
celebrated with joy."[9] It is this kind of thankfulness that is vital to the
Christian life, for it transforms our perspective from earthbound to
God-focused.

The Question Again

What do I have that I did not receive? As I survey all that I've been
given by God the Father and reflect on who I've become through
my union with Christ and by the transforming work of His Spirit, I
realize that this inventory activity will never be done. For as long as
I live, I can keep counting and treasuring, and the task will still not
be completed.

Even so, holding my unfinished inventory spreadsheet in hand,
I understand that I have received *everything*. I humbly acknowledge
that all of it is a gift. Because I am always tempted to glory in myself,
I need to regularly hear God's wise command to give thanks to Him.
Being by nature ungrateful and discontent, I need the gracious help
of God's Spirit to move me to worship and praise. For I confess that
even this slowly growing grateful spirit is a gift. Even this life of
imperfect thanksgiving has been granted to me by God. To Him be
all thanksgiving and honor, forever and ever!

---

8. John Baillie, *The Sense of the Presence of God* (New York: Scribner, 1962), 72.
9. Henri J. M. Nouwen, *The Return of the Prodigal Son* (New York: Doubleday, 1992), 85.

Reflect . . .

- ◆ So, what about you? What do you have that you did not receive?

- ◆ Just to unpack the question: What do you have?

- ◆ Of everything you have, how much was given to you?

- ◆ To whom will you be thankful?

- ◆ How will you show Him your thanks?

CHAPTER 2

The Good and Gracious Giver

Few Christian writers have graced us with more pithy quotations about thanksgiving than G. K. Chesterton. This was the man who memorably expressed "the chief idea" of his life in this way: "When it comes to life, the critical thing is whether you take things for granted or take them with gratitude."[1]

Another perceptive Chestertonian observation introduces the focus of this chapter: "The worst moment for the atheist is when he is really thankful and has no one to thank."[2] The notion of being blessed or feeling indebted requires that some other person be thanked. Gratitude searches for a worthy object. But for someone who does not believe in the true God or worship Him, where should the response of gratitude be directed? To whom shall I present my thanks?

To Whom Will We Be Thankful?
The sad plight of the thankful atheist is nothing new. In the previous chapter, I mentioned the curious rise of God-less thanksgiving and unholy gratitude. People want to be thankful, but they resort to thanking themselves, good luck, or something else. Fyodor

---

1. G. K. Chesterton, *The Autobiography of G. K. Chesterton* (New York: Sheed & Ward, 1936), 341–42.

2. G. K. Chesterton, *St. Francis of Assisi* (Garden City, N.Y.: Image Books, 1957), 78.

Dostoevsky lived in a time and culture when the Christian faith—
indeed, all theistic faith—was being suppressed and discarded. And
Dostoevsky too was concerned for humankind if God was not there
to be thanked: "Who is man going to love then?" his character Dimitri asks in *The Brothers Karamazov*. "To whom will he be thankful?
To whom will he sing the hymn?" To the idea that "one can love
humanity instead of God," Dimitri responds that "only an idiot can
maintain that."[3]

There is an almost irrepressible feeling of gratitude in the human
heart. Yet we don't want to recognize the Giver because to recognize God requires that we worship and obey Him. And from the
moment that sin entered the world, the fool has been saying in his
heart, "There is no God" (Ps. 14:1). Consequently, the thankfulness
that casts about for an earthly object can hardly be termed *gratitude*
at all. The appreciation-filled and gratitude-journaling person who
does not bow before God in thanksgiving is a person who will not
thrive, not as long as he or she lives in rebellion against God.

In fact, ingratitude is part of the basic equipment of sinful humankind. It is striking that in Romans 1, when Paul begins to describe
our total depravity, ingratitude is prominent among our damning
sins. God's glorious existence is plainly evident in His works in the
creation and preservation of the universe, yet humankind has withheld worship from God. Instead, we have turned against Him in
unbelief and idolatry.

Humankind's response to the Lord has been wholly wrong. Says
Paul, "Although they knew God, they did not glorify Him as God,
nor were thankful, but became futile in their thoughts, and their
foolish hearts were darkened" (Rom. 1:21). Despite receiving innumerable gifts from the Creator—life, physical strength, daily bread,
the knowledge of God's moral requirements, the possibility of eternal fellowship with God—our first parents did not glorify God or

3. Fyodor Dostoevsky, *The Brothers Karamazov*, trans. Constance Garnett, ed.
Manuel Komroff, Signet Classics (New York: New American Library, 1958), 685.

thank Him. They rejected the Giver and corrupted His good gifts. They were ungrateful.

This is the continued failure of sinful humankind. Within the human heart is an innate awareness of a giver, some benefactor. Yet we are inclined to corrupt and idolize created things. It is probably not too much to say that "all sin is ingratitude—refusing to thank God for what he has given and wanting, ungratefully, what he has not."[4]

Apart from God's gracious help, we will persist in the most blameworthy ingratitude. Apart from God's powerful resetting of our focus, humankind will forever fixate on the gifts and withhold worship from the Giver. Here is what Dostoevsky said about humanity: "If he is not stupid, he is monstrously ungrateful! Phenomenally ungrateful. In fact, I believe that the best definition of man is the ungrateful biped."[5]

The Object of Gratitude

For whom should a thankful atheist seek? Or where can naturally ungrateful bipeds like us trudge with that stubborn urge to thank someone? Gratitude needs an appropriate target. And the right target is the Giver who has been richly generous.

James 1:17 contains a truth that is fundamental to the aims of this book. It also suggests the thanksgiving that should characterize the lives of God's children: "Every good gift and every perfect gift is from above, and comes down from the Father of lights, with whom there is no variation or shadow of turning." James points to the source of every gift that we have received: our glorious heavenly Father, who is unchanging in His perfections. It is in God's very nature to be generous and giving toward His creatures.

4. A. William DeJong, *Eucharistic Reciprocity: A Practical Theological Inquiry into the Virtue of Gratitude* (Eugene, Ore.: Pickwick, 2019), 202.

5. Fyodor Dostoevsky, *Notes from Underground, The Double and Other Stories*, trans. Constance Garnett, Barnes and Noble Classics (New York: Barnes and Noble Books, 2003), 257.

True thankfulness keeps our focus on God as we daily respond to His goodness and grace. Our grateful spirits are enriched as we meditate on the triune God as the source of the many good gifts we have received. In fact, the more we express our gratitude to Him, the more our eyes will be opened to His constant kindness. To explore the character of God as the Giver, we'll focus on His attributes of goodness and grace.

God Is Good

Students of the Bible know that the command repeated most often in Scripture is God's settling word to His people: "Do not fear." A command heard less often but still with notable frequency is this: "Give thanks to the LORD, for He is good!" (see, e.g., Ps. 136:1). This scriptural exhortation is likewise a refrain throughout this book, because it encourages us to give thanks to the Lord. For now, we want to highlight God's glorious character as it is celebrated in this thankful chorus: "Give thanks to the LORD, for He is *good*."

The goodness of God is a description of His essential character. To say that God is good means that God is not evil or unjust, but utterly benevolent and unchangeably generous. Indeed, "God has in himself an infinite and inexhaustible treasure of all blessedness, enough to fill all things."[6]

As with all His perfections, God's goodness is not a theoretical concept but a living truth. God is pleased to express His goodness through His deeds and purposes here on earth. The psalmist tightly connects divine character with divine activity when he sings to the Lord in Psalm 119:68, "You are good, and *do* good."

In the same spirit, Scripture speaks enthusiastically about God as the source of goodness. For instance, David in Psalm 36 says that God brings many blessings on His people: "They are abundantly satisfied with the fullness of Your house, and You give them drink from the river of Your pleasures" (v. 8). God provides for His thirsty people, allowing us to kneel at His bounteous river and be satisfied.

---

6. A. W. Pink, *The Attributes of God* (Grand Rapids: Baker, 1975), 74.

David builds on the image of God as a bubbling source of water in the next verse: "For with You is the fountain of life" (v. 9). We are accustomed to finding fountains in carefully controlled settings like parks, swimming pools, and splash pads. But a true fountain is more than a stream of water that looks attractive to passersby or provides enjoyment for children on a hot day. A true fountain is a source of water from the depths of the earth. Such is God: the fountain of life, the source of unending goodness.

The scriptural portrait of God's goodness is beautifully captured by the Belgic Confession (1561) when it describes God as the "overflowing fountain of all good" (art. 1). The descriptor *overflowing* expresses the truth that in all our requesting and receiving, we cannot exhaust God. He cannot be drained by our constant need. If we trust Him and seek Him with our whole heart, we will never walk away from God unsatisfied. And if our eyes are opened to His goodness, we'll come to see what Jeremiah describes in Lamentations 3:

> Through the LORD's mercies we are not consumed,
> Because His compassions fail not.
> They are new every morning;
> Great is Your faithfulness. (vv. 22–23)

God's mercies endure, His compassions never fail, and His goodness is new every morning.

God's ever-new goodness teaches us to value His gifts afresh each day. Many of us have always enjoyed three good meals a day, had a comfortable house to inhabit, and had people in our life to love. Perhaps many of us have long known Jesus as our Savior and always have been strengthened by His Spirit within us. These blessings are familiar, yet they should retain their brightness in our minds and hearts. Truly, these gifts are "new every morning." As we arise every morning, we step into a world that the good God is preserving and governing. Every morning, we are allowed to begin a new day that our Father has prepared for us.

Filled by God, "the fountain of life," we can say with David,

My cup runs over.
Surely goodness and mercy shall follow me
All the days of my life. (Ps. 23:5–6)

The Lord sends constant blessing because that is who God is. His goodness endures, never depleted and never diminished. We come to the overflowing fountain empty-handed yet boldly, knowing that this good God will surely answer. Says Psalm 31:19, "Oh, how great is Your goodness, which You have laid up for those who fear You." God's goodness abounds, and my cup overflows.

He Is Good to All
This goodness of God extends widely. Far from being restricted to the realm of humankind or His church, God demonstrates generosity throughout His world, for He sustains all creatures, great and small. David confesses:

The eyes of all look expectantly to You,
And You give them their food in due season.
You open Your hand
And satisfy the desire of every living thing.
    (Ps. 145:15–16)

As the recipients of His daily gifts, all God's creatures experience His goodness. He gives the needed food and drink for survival, allows flourishing, and grants a steady increase (see Ps. 104:10–30).

In a striking passage, Isaiah actually points to domestic livestock, who acknowledge their benefactors, as an example to the ungrateful Israelites:

The ox knows its owner
And the donkey its master's crib;
But Israel does not know,
My people do not consider. (Isa. 1:3)

God provides for the wild animals that inhabit the oceans, skies, and wildernesses of the earth, and He also provides for oxen, donkeys, cats, and goldfish through the care of their owners. Such animals are quickly conditioned to expect good things from the hand of humans. Take our family dog, for instance. Maple always loves to be near us. We like to think that this is because of the warmth of our personalities. But it is really because she recognizes that these bipeds control the resources for which she is ever hungry. You might say that our dog is thankful to us—at the very least, like the ox and donkey of Isaiah 1, she understands the true source of her blessings. By contrast, how often do we forget where it all comes from? How often do we fail to consider that we have our being only through the daily goodness of the Lord? "Israel does not know, My people do not consider."

But God's goodness is a deep fountain. While God shows goodness toward His creatures generally, His goodness is seen particularly in His disposition toward those who bear His image. When we sinned against Him and began to worship created things rather than the Creator, God, in His holy wrath, did not destroy us. Nor did He deprive us of every good thing like we deserved. Instead, God saw fit to promise, engineer, and then accomplish the salvation of sinners through the indescribable gift of Jesus Christ. As Mark Jones puts it, "God's goodness provides the reason why God redeemed men and women through his Son."[7]

God's gifts to His creation are richly varied, but this blessing of salvation belongs in a category entirely on its own. In Christ, sinners are allowed to possess sure and everlasting redemption as "the highest gift possible for the Father to bestow on his people."[8] This gift can never be outdone. And while an ox knows its owner and a dog lovingly licks the hand that feeds her, it is humankind alone who receives the ability to express heartfelt gratitude to God. In thanksgiving we humbly remember His past mercies and offer up joyful worship to His name.

---

7. Mark Jones, *God Is: A Devotional Guide to the Attributes of God* (Wheaton, Ill.: Crossway, 2017), 137.

8. Jones, *God Is*, 139.

A Psalm of Thanksgiving

Psalm 100 voices the thankful response of the redeemed for God's many gifts. While numerous psalms ascribe thanks and praise to God, Psalm 100 is unique in being expressly dedicated to gratitude. The superscription says it is "A Psalm of Thanksgiving." This brief psalm is marked by a jubilant tone of thankfulness to the Lord. Consider verse 2: "Serve the LORD with gladness; come before His presence with singing."

This psalm of thanksgiving urges everyone to worship the Lord and emphasizes this call by declaring the grounds for worship. Chief among the reasons for heartfelt gratitude to God is that the Lord has created and saved Israel. Consequently, Israel belongs to God, and they are His beloved flock: "It is He who has made us, and not we ourselves; we are His people and the sheep of His pasture" (v. 3). Israel owes their very existence to Him, from the moment of their creation, to their redemption from captivity, to their ongoing preservation. The psalm rejoices to affirm, "We are His people."

How, then, should God's people answer His great deeds? By thanking God! The psalm invites us to "make a joyful shout to the LORD" (v. 1), to serve Him with gladness (v. 2), and to come before Him with singing (v. 2). In the thematic verse 4, the psalmist exhorts the redeemed to respond to God with thankfulness:

> Enter into His gates with *thanksgiving*,
> And into His courts with praise.
> Be *thankful* to Him, and bless His name.

The people who know themselves to be chosen and saved by God will be grateful. And those who are grateful will be busy with worship and praise.

Psalm 100 describes the activity of God's people in responding to His goodness. But the psalm centers the worshipers' attention on the *object* of their thankful praise: the Lord God. The opening cry in verse 1 calls us to "Make a joyful shout to the LORD." Then verse 5 declares,

The LORD is good;
His mercy is everlasting,
And His truth endures to all generations.

From beginning to end, it extols the enduringly good God as the
worthy recipient of praise. Goldingay notes of this psalm, "Theo-
logically, its central affirmation is 'Yhwh—he is God.'"[9] Psalm 100
teaches us that true thanksgiving always springs from knowing and
loving the Lord as our good God.

Loving the Good God
Meditating on God's attributes elicits a worshipful response. As we
ponder the goodness of the Lord, we remember again the true origin
of every blessing. The clothing we wear, our job, our church family,
the gospel that we treasure—from where has it all come but from the
overflowing fountain of all that is good? And so we cheerfully echo
the Psalm 100 praise: "Be thankful to Him, and bless His name. For
the LORD is good" (vv. 4–5).

Those who often marvel at God's goodness become transformed
by it. It has always been the Lord's will that His glory gets reflected in
His creation. Consider how in the beginning, the flawless universe
He crafted was a testimony to His goodness; it was all "very good"
(Gen. 1:31). And though the creation is now broken and humankind
is fallen, God is renewing us in His image. Paul says in Ephesians
4:24 that God is reshaping us in "true righteousness and holiness,"
and, we might add, reshaping us in true goodness. As John writes,
"He who does good is of God" (3 John 11). Sinners who love the
good God begin to reflect God's goodness. We do so by showing generosity toward our neighbors, promoting the welfare of those who
suffer, and serving faithfully with His gifts. In thankfulness to Him,
we strive to be and to do good, as God is good.

If you have tasted and seen that the Lord is good, has His goodness sunk deeply into your life? Are you a person who is eager to

9. John Goldingay, *Psalms: Baker Commentary on the Old Testament Wisdom
and Psalms* (Grand Rapids: Baker Academic, 2006), 3:137.

do good to everyone, especially those of the household of faith (Gal. 6:10)? By a daily dependence on God's enduring goodness, do you strive not to become weary in doing good (v. 9)? Are people able to see your good works and so give glory to God the Father (Matt. 5:16)?

God Is Gracious

Many years ago, long before I entered the ministry, I heard someone talking about what constituted a good sermon. His expectation was that every sermon include the word *grace*. If the preacher mentioned God's grace at least once, then it could probably be considered a good sermon. As a preacher, I have sometimes wished that crafting a good sermon was as easy as adding a generous dash of a favorite theological term, maybe *grace* or *covenant* or *election* or something else. Proper preaching requires more than a nod to biblical word studies or subculture shibboleths. Still, grace is a vital ingredient! For the gospel, nothing is more fundamental than grace. Grace is the heart of what we preach when we preach Christ. Grace is the foundation of what we believe when we believe in Jesus.

What made the Father willing to send a Savior? Or what moves God to send us daily gifts? The answer resides in that single word *grace*. This is the eternal and free favor of God, shown in His spiritual and eternal blessings on the guilty and unworthy. For lack of a more refined way to phrase it, grace is given us "just because"—just because of who God is. This is His character, the quality of His being. Says A.W. Pink, "Divine grace is the sovereign and saving favor of God exercised in the bestowment of blessings upon those who have no merit *in* them and for which no compensation is demanded *from* them."[10] By definition, grace cannot be bought, earned, or won.

We see the eminence of grace throughout Scripture, where it sums up all the benefits that come to us from God through Christ. Consider the beloved text in Ephesians 2:8: "For by grace you have been saved through faith, and that not of yourselves, it is the gift of

---

10. Pink, *Attributes of God*, 84–85; emphasis original.

God." Here *grace* is associated with a gift. Salvation was impossible to secure, inaccessible and out of reach. But God was graciously willing to be favorable toward us and to act for our benefit. His kindness is not something that we have deserved, not something on which we have a claim, yet it is generously bestowed. His grace is the blessed root of the manifold gifts we have received.

And so we like to say, "There, but for the grace of God, go I!" This is not so different from what Paul writes in 1 Corinthians 15:10: "By the grace of God I am what I am." It was solely God's grace that transformed Paul from the chief of sinners to the apostle of God's glory in Christ. God's grace likewise transforms us, turning us from beggars and orphans into royal children.

The Fullness of Grace

In the first chapter of his gospel, John sketches the cosmic drama of salvation. Jesus came to this world as one who was God Himself, the one through whom all things were made. Taking on human flesh, Jesus arrived to accomplish salvation through His blood and to create a new family for God.

And the sole basis for this amazing redemptive work is God's grace. John wants to emphasize that there is nothing lacking about it, for he says twice that God's grace in Christ is "full." He says of Jesus, "We beheld His glory, the glory as of the only begotten of the Father, *full* of grace and truth" (John 1:14). And again in verse 16 he says, "Of His *fullness* we have all received, and grace for grace." When God gives grace, He does not reluctantly open a finger to allow some to trickle out. He is openhanded and provides us with every good thing we need. As a gracious Father, He pours out gifts on His beloved. As a good Father, He shows generosity to His children.

We have become God's own family members, His little ones. In His holy house He welcomes us to a lavish feast where we are filled to overflowing. As John puts it, "And of His fullness we have all received, and grace for grace" (1:16). In English it is hard to capture the sense of the original Greek of verse 16. But John says something like this: "From His fullness we have received *grace in exchange for grace.*" It is a stunning picture of God's largesse. It depicts God not simply heaping up a pile of blessings for us, each new gift atop the last. That would be good, but this is even better. When God gives one blessing, then gives another to take its place—a fresh blessing—it is brand new: "grace in exchange for grace."

Perhaps you have stood at the seaside and watched the mesmerizing spectacle of the waves. They rise out of the water, gather in size and speed, and then crash on the shore. Hour by hour the waves keep coming, steady and unstoppable, yet they never accumulate. No heap of waves litters the shore because the waves are always new. So it is for God's grace in Christ: it keeps coming. One blessing from God is a sure promise that the next one is not far behind. As the New International Version puts verse 16, "Out of his fullness we have all received grace in place of grace already given." The grace of God never ebbs but always flows.

There may come seasons when we wonder if God's grace has subsided. We might hit a dry spell, when His gifts seem few and far between. But Scripture teaches us to have eyes that are open for the tokens of His favor. It may be only a small blessing, a gift that appears insignificant. In the middle of your bleak weak, it may be the blessing of an uplifting song, a warm conversation, a satisfying meal, a heartening time of devotion. It is just one small wave, but where there is one, another is sure to follow.

From God's fullness will always flow new gifts. With open eyes and open hands, we may receive each small gift as another gesture of God's love in Christ. Each fatherly blessing is another proof that He will keep giving. For as long as we live, even for eternity, we will keep receiving. Where have you seen God's grace today?

Being Gracious

It is God's amazing grace that motivates, stimulates, and prompts our thanksgiving. In Titus 2 Paul describes how the saving grace of God frees our life from the futility of sin. Instead, His grace repurposes us for leading righteous and godly lives that are filled with good works: "For the grace of God that brings salvation has appeared to all men, teaching us that, denying ungodliness and worldly lusts, we should live soberly, righteously, and godly in the present age…that [Christ] might redeem us from every lawless deed and purify for Himself His own special people, zealous for good works" (vv. 11–12, 14). Scripture's thanksgiving refrain expresses this same movement from divine grace to human gratitude: "Give thanks to the LORD, for He is good! For His mercy endures forever" (Ps. 136:1). While mercy is not identical to grace, it is conceptually similar. Children of God have received unexpected and unfailing kindness. They respond by giving thanks to the Lord.

Even the words used by the Holy Spirit demonstrate that gratitude is the right response to grace. The Greek word for grace is *charis*, while the Greek word for gratitude is built on the same root: *eucharistia*. This tight connection is seen, for example, in how "saying grace" at mealtimes is equivalent to offering a prayer of thanksgiving. Bryan Chapell explains how this worshipful attitude grows among those who have received the gift of salvation: "The heart that knows grace longs to thank God for his mercy.… This is not an imposed pattern; it is the reflex response of the heart that has grasped the gospel."[11]

And so it is right for a child of God to reflect on the impact of His grace on his or her life. Are you grateful for grace? Are you grace-filled? Sometimes we describe a person who is exceptionally patient and kind and generous as gracious. But no child of God should be a stranger to this description. Divine grace is irresistibly transformative. We will consider this more in a later chapter, but it is right to reflect: Has God's abounding grace made you a gracious person? As you have received God's many gifts, how have you been using them to bless others?

Conclusion: Our Generous God

We have admired two attributes of God in relation to the theme of thanksgiving. We end by considering His generosity. What does it

---

11. Bryan Chapell, *Christ-Centered Worship* (Grand Rapids: Baker Academic, 2009), 92.

mean to be generous? It is readiness to give more than is necessary or expected. A generous person doesn't simply give but *keeps* giving. Even when someone thinks that she has contributed enough, she continues to give. That is the nature of God: He is good, He is gracious, and He is generous, the source of every good and perfect gift (James 1:17).

In Psalm 52:1 David confesses, "The goodness of God endures continually." The Lord's favor toward His people continues always. It is never diminished. People speak of donor fatigue these days, when folks no longer wish to give charitably because they have already given a lot, motivation has waned, or resources have dwindled. But our God is not a man, that He should tire of giving. God keeps giving because we keep needing. As Paul reminds the Philippians, "My God shall supply all your need according to His riches in glory by Christ Jesus" (Phil. 4:19).

Because He is a generous Father, God delights to give good gifts to His children. So Scripture instructs us not to "trust in uncertain riches but in the living God, who gives us richly all things to enjoy" (1 Tim. 6:17). This is a reminder not to fixate on earthly things as the most valuable feature of our life. Rather, we should put our trust in the living God, who blesses us in His goodness and grace. Learn to rest in the God who gives us "richly all things to enjoy." The rich plenitude of God's generosity is captured in this beautiful prayer of thanksgiving:

> O Lord my God,
>   for life and reason, nurture, preservation, guidance,
>   education;
>   for Thy gifts of grace and nature,
>   for Thy calling, recalling, manifold recalling me again
>   and again;
>   for Thy forbearance, long-suffering, and long long-
>   suffering toward me, even until now;
>   for all from whom I have received any good or help;
>   for the use of Thy present good things;
>   for Thy promise, and my hope, of good things to come;

for all these things, and for all other, which I know,
which I know not, manifest or
secret, remembered or forgotten by me, I praise
Thee, I bless Thee, I give Thee thanks;
and I will praise, and bless, and give Thee thanks, all
the days of my life.
What shall I render unto the Lord for all His benefits
to me?
Thou art worthy, O Lord, to receive glory, and honor,
and power—Amen.[12]

Reflect . . .

- Before praying, it is good to reflect for a moment: What good gifts have you recently enjoyed?

- To be truly grateful, we need to truly know the Giver. Do you know God in His goodness and grace?

- To whom, then, will you present your thanks?

- In your life, how have you experienced God's generosity to be never failing and never depleted?

- And how do you thank God?

---

12. Lancelot Andrewes, in *Prayers Ancient and Modern*, ed. Mary Wilder Tiletson (New York: Grosset & Dunlap, 1928), 99.

CHAPTER 3

God's Ground for Giving

Our thankfulness to God has one motivation more profound than any other. It arises by considering the reason why God has been so good toward us. To echo David's words when the Lord promised to establish His house and kingdom, "Who am I, O Lord GOD? And what is my house, that You have brought me this far?" (2 Sam. 7:18). David was overwhelmed with God's kindness. He struggled to fathom how and why the Lord would do such good for him, a mere man and lowly sinner.

Who Am I, O Lord God?

Do you ever ask a question like David's? Who am I, that God has been so good to me? Why all this goodness? After reflecting on what you have that you did not receive—and when seeing that you received everything, from the oxygen in your lungs, to the credit card in your wallet, to the everlasting inheritance of salvation—it is good and right to ponder why God has seen fit to shower His blessings.

This question becomes weightier when we think about what God owes us. What are you entitled to? What is God obligated to provide for your enjoyment? Because of our sinfulness, we have earned not a single blessing. Instead, we have merited the holy God's condemnation. Recall that by nature we are a willfully ungrateful people (Rom. 1:21). We are inclined to be rebellious against God our Creator (v. 25), and so we are deserving of eternal death (v. 32).

By nature, we stand empty-handed before God. In ourselves, we are impoverished of every good thing and lack all prospect of improvement. Yet God is generous in giving. Says Watts, "We are as vile and unworthy as others, and our God beholds all our unworthiness, all our guilt, our repeated provocations, and his past mercies abused, and yet he continues to have mercy upon us and waits to be gracious."[1]

The Supreme Ground

It belongs to the holy character of God to give liberally. He even blesses those who do not willingly submit to Him. Jesus says about God the Father, "He makes His sun rise on the evil and on the good, and sends rain on the just and on the unjust" (Matt. 5:45). In being so generous, God's purpose is that all people acknowledge Him.

Paul once explained this liberality to the Athenians. He told them that God "gives to all life, breath, and all things," with the purpose that everyone "should seek the Lord, in the hope that they might grope for Him and find Him, though He is not far from each one of us" (Acts 17:25, 27). And in the same address, the apostle announced the sole basis of God's restored fellowship with sinners: "the Man whom He has ordained" (v. 31). Jesus Christ has opened the way for us back to God the Creator.

In Christ we have our greatest treasure. When Paul in 2 Corinthians 9:15 says, "Thanks be to God for His indescribable gift!" the principal gift of which he is thinking is Christ. Only because we have Jesus do we have anything good, and only because of Him has God become our gracious Father. Don Whitney writes, "It is no burden to serve God when we consider what great things He has done for us."[2] Christ's gift of salvation must move us to a life of thanksgiving. He is the one who restores our thanksgiving.

1. Isaac Watts, *A Guide to Prayer* (Edinburgh: Banner of Truth, 2001), 32.
2. Donald S. Whitney, *Spiritual Disciplines for the Christian Life* (Colorado Springs: NavPress, 1991), 112.

The One Who Restores Our Thanksgiving

An ass is often more appreciative than a human. Remember how God voiced this complaint about Israel (Isa. 1:3). The Lord had treated His covenant people with generosity, yet the prophet laments their deep and persistent ingratitude, announcing that God will righteously withhold His good gifts for a time.

During the period in which Isaiah was ministering, the people of Judah witnessed their northern neighbors, the ten tribes of Israel, removed to Assyria. These were their fellow citizens, cousins and uncles and extended family, and they would never return. But though Judah had been spared for a time, she could not rest easy behind Jerusalem's thick stone walls. Isaiah speaks about the same terrifying judgment that will come if they continue in breaking God's commands. And the outlook is grim, for they will not change their ways.

And so Isaiah announces that armies will invade the land and besiege Jerusalem. Her walls will be breached and toppled. The holy temple will be filled not with the smoke of God's glory, but the smoke of its burning timbers. Families will walk not on a happy pilgrimage, but on a miserable trek into exile. For a large part of Isaiah's prophecy, he must bring a fearful message of death and destruction, executions and exile.

Yet with the God of all grace, there is always hope. After a long season of loss and grief, God will allow a remnant to return. As the crucial basis for this new beginning, someone will atone for the people's sin. Isaiah announces the appearance of a Suffering Servant, the Messiah, to bear iniquities, restore peace, and heal the land.

And notably, the expected Christ will reestablish thanksgiving in Israel. Isaiah prophesies in chapter 51,

> For the LORD will comfort Zion,
> He will comfort all her waste places;
> He will make her wilderness like Eden,
> And her desert like the garden of the LORD;
> Joy and gladness will be found in it,
> *Thanksgiving* and the voice of melody. (v. 3)

The people who once walked in unthankfulness will again know the great gift of gratitude. Not only will God give them an incredible reason for thankfulness, but He will also give a thankful spirit. In the Messiah's land, there will be joy and gladness, singing and thanksgiving.

Complete in Christ

From the very first chapters of the New Testament, it is clear that the One whom Isaiah prophesied about has come (Matt. 1:22–23). His name is Immanuel, Jesus, the Christ. After His ministry, death, resurrection, and ascension into heaven, the apostles expounded the meaning and importance of Christ.

In his letter to the church of Colossae, for example, Paul is busy with two closely related purposes. His first purpose is to warn against a heresy that included the deadly strain of legalism. This is the notion that says God will bless us because we adhere to a code of conduct, a set of guidelines or traditions. God loves us because we have been doing well at keeping the rules.

Legalism is dangerous for all kinds of reasons. But it has one especially terrible side effect: it renders unnecessary the person and work of Christ! Who needs Christ's deliverance if we can pull ourselves out of the muck of sin? Who needs the good news if you have sufficient goodness of your own? It is frustratingly hard not to harbor the quiet thought that we have earned our good things. When I look at what I have, it's a product of my hard work. And doesn't God owe me a little something because of how I have faithfully served Him?

To refute the false teachers, Paul does a second thing in his letter: he insists on the preeminence of Jesus Christ as the sole basis for redemption. He exalts Christ as the only alternative to failed do-it-yourself schemes. In Colossians, Paul piles up the praise for Christ. He is the Creator of the universe (Col. 1:16), the Sustainer of all things, and in Him all things hold together (v. 17). Christ is the head of the church (v. 18) and the fullness of God in bodily form (v. 19). What is more, Christ has rescued us from the power of darkness and brought us into the kingdom of light (v. 13). In Him we have redemption through His blood, the forgiveness of sins (v. 14).

At the cross, Jesus dealt with the sin that separates us from God our Creator. Through Christ, sin is pardoned, evil is conquered, and God gives a new righteousness and holiness. By Him we have free access to God's glorious presence in prayer and worship. So Paul says to the Colossians, "You are complete in Him" (2:10). If you behold Scripture's astounding picture of Christ, there can be no one who says, "But He is not enough. Something is missing, and I need more than Jesus." Christ has no shortcoming and no deficiency. The antidote to false teaching, the guard against this world's seduction—and the surefire motivation to true gratitude—always comes through embracing the fullness of life in God the Son.

Receiving the Real Gift

In seeking to promote the grateful worship of God, Paul reminds the Colossians, and he reminds us, "You…have received Christ Jesus the Lord" (2:6). To be sure, we may want to receive many other things besides Him. In fact, we often connect our gratitude directly to an inventory of gifts and blessings: "I am thankful to God because I received a promotion or had a profitable year at work." "I am thankful because I received a child or a grandchild." "I am thankful to receive a clean bill of health."

We should indeed be grateful for everything received, and this book will press you to tally and treasure God's many good gifts. But in them we must not expect to find completeness or satisfaction. All these things are not the greatest prize—only Christ is. You have received *Him*!

Compare it to the child who gets a special birthday gift from her parents. Much thought went into the gift, and it was purchased at a significant cost. Dad and Mom are excited by how much their child will enjoy the present. But what happens when she opens it? She glances at the gift, plays with it halfheartedly for a while, then spends all morning happily playing with the big box in which it came. In

her simplicity, she missed the point. She didn't realize what the real
gift was.

We smile at a child who is happy with a cardboard box. But God
calls us all to return to what is really important. Through its promises and stories and prayers, Scripture reorders the list of priorities
that we maintain, resets our mental bookmarks on the things we
value. We easily forget what is truly essential. Our attention is soon
diverted to something far less important, far less valuable, far less
beautiful than Christ.

But what is God's central and primary gift? We have received
Christ. The fullness of God's Son fills our emptiness, for we "are
complete in Him" (Col. 2:10). He is much more than any material
possession, earthly position, relationship, memory, or skill that you
might value. When you are united to Christ by faith, you have the
real gift and the real reason to live in thanksgiving. It is when we
foster a delight in Christ that gratitude grows.

Surely this is why, immediately after declaring our completeness
in Christ, Paul calls us to a thankful response: "As you therefore have
received Christ Jesus the Lord, so walk in Him, rooted and built up
in Him and established in the faith, as you have been taught, *abounding in it with thanksgiving*" (Col. 2:6–7). Sinners who were worthy
of condemnation but who are now welcomed by the Father should
abound in thanksgiving. Luther exhorts us, "See that you do not forget what you were before, lest you take for granted the grace and
mercy you received from God and forget to express your gratitude
each day."[3]

And All Things

You have received Christ. And what about everything else you were
hoping to receive? God promises that He will also provide whatever
is truly needed. Consider the glorious logic of Romans 8:32: "He
who did not spare His own Son, but delivered Him up for us all,

3. As quoted in R. T. Kendall, *Thanking God* (London: Hodder & Stoughton,
2003), 19.

how shall He not with Him also freely give us all things?" This was no small gift or inconsequential offering: God did not spare His *own* Son but was willing to give Him up for vile sinners, even for a people yet to be born or believe.

You don't need to be a parent to stand amazed at such love. Jesus was the Father's only and perfect Son, yet the Father was willing not just to let evil men vent their cruel anger on Him but took an active role in His Son's suffering. He exercised the full power of His wrath against Christ, not relenting or having mercy, not until the suffering was done and the price was paid. God did not spare His own Son but gave Him up for us all.

Ephesians 3:18–19 says that in Christ we may begin to see how wide and long and deep and high God's love is. If we ponder the universe, looking at the limitless sky above and the infinite horizon on every side and the depth of the earth and seas beneath us, we may quietly say, "That is what the love of God in Christ is like." His love is deeper than our guilt, wider than our worries, longer than our sadness, and higher than all our fears. There is no person who can be outside the love of God, and there is no place outside His reach.

Seeing the price paid, we are assured of the Father's preservation. How could God ever give us up? After engineering such a costly salvation, how could He let us fall away due to human weakness, worldly trouble, or satanic temptation?

And then consider again Paul's question: "He who did not spare His own Son, but delivered Him up for us all, *how shall He not with Him also freely give us all things*?" (Rom. 8:32). Marvel at his question's beautiful logic. It goes like this: Beyond any doubt, God proved His love at the cross, where He loved us to the greatest extent by giving His Son. Now we have His promise that together with Christ, God will give "all things." If God has already given so much through Christ, what is a little more? If God has already afforded you eternal salvation, won't He supply you with every other thing you need? Will He not also give faith, wisdom, and daily bread? He will.

· This promise of God's love rings true when we sin, when we stray, when we are anxious about the future, or when we are burdened

with the cares of our family. This promise of God's love is true even
when God seems far away—God will not abandon us, for He paid
too much. "Gratitude reminds us that, in God's economy of gifts,
everything is free because it cost Christ everything. Nothing for us is
earned and nothing is deserved."[4]

We are empty-handed beggars who have been lavishly filled. We
are crimson-hued sinners washed whiter than snow. We have God's
promise, backed up and confirmed in Christ: "For all the promises of
God in Him are Yes, and in Him Amen, to the glory of God through
us" (2 Cor. 1:20). And God has reinforced the foundation of our
thanksgiving in Christ by giving us His meal of thanksgiving.

Christ's Thanksgiving Meal

Many people love a thanksgiving feast of turkey, ham, and starchy
carbohydrates. But the ultimate thanksgiving feast was given to us
by Christ on the night He was betrayed. In Reformed churches, it is
called the Holy Supper, the Lord's Supper, or Communion. Another
name is the Eucharist, the Greek name first applied to the sacrament
by the church father Ignatius many centuries ago.

What does *Eucharist* mean? Essentially, it means "thanksgiving,"
which is a scriptural way of speaking about this sacrament. When
instructing the Corinthians about the Lord's Supper, Paul asks, "The
cup of blessing which we bless, is it not the communion of the blood
of Christ?" (1 Cor. 10:16). In the Greek he says literally, "The cup
of blessing for which we give *thanks*." Jesus demonstrated this spirit
by offering two prayers of thanksgiving at the first Eucharist. Peter
Leithart observes, "Jesus graced the dreadful evening of his betrayal
with gratitude."[5]

At the Lord's meal in Christian churches today, the focus ought
to be on giving thanks to God. Thanksgiving is the joyous atmosphere at the Lord's Table because of the covenant fellowship we

---

4. DeJong, *Eucharistic Reciprocity*, 236.
5. Peter J. Leithart, *Gratitude: An Intellectual History* (Waco, Tex.: Baylor University Press, 2014), 34.

may enjoy with God through Christ. There is no greater blessing, no greater gift, than His one sacrifice. Jesus's saving grace (Greek: *charis*) for which we give thanks to God (Greek: *eucharistia*) is celebrated in the Eucharist.

If we examine 1 Corinthians 10:16 more closely, we see in the background a familiar scene from Jewish homes. It was a custom that at the end of a meal, thanksgiving would be spoken to God for the food and drink. The father would pronounce a prayer of thanks: "God of heaven and earth, we thank You for all Your gifts."

Because thanksgiving was offered at every meal, it was fitting that it also be done at the Passover meal. Once a year, Jewish families would remember God's great deeds of salvation in delivering them from Egypt (Ex. 12:1–28). A tradition developed that at different times during the Passover meal, four cups of wine would be passed around the table. The fourth cup of wine, shared after the food had been eaten, was called the cup of blessing, for it accompanied the final prayer of thanksgiving. It was probably this cup that Jesus lifted up and blessed at the Last Supper (1 Cor. 11:25). This was the high point of the meal, the moment when Jesus reveals Himself as the true Passover sacrifice.

Believers today are allowed to receive the same cup of blessing. We may receive His cup with deep gratitude and unshakable joy. In this cup is Christ's blood of the covenant poured out for many for the forgiveness of sins (Matt. 26:27–28). We receive from His hand the cup of salvation, rich and full of Christ's benefits (Ps. 116:13).

So what should we do with the cup Christ gives us at His feast? Note again what Paul says: it is "the cup of thanksgiving *for which we give thanks*" (1 Cor. 10:16 NIV). Such gratitude is not just a task for Communion Sunday; it is the calling of a lifetime. After Christ gives you the cup, give thanks to Him. He is the enduring foundation and the enlivening motivation for all our gratitude.

Thank Him with your songs of praise—let psalms and hymns give voice to the gratitude of your heart. Thank God with your financial gifts, cheerfully given to serve others. Thank God through your prayers, adoring and loving and honoring God for who He is.

Thank God with a love for other people that resembles God's love for us. Thank God with your holiness by rejecting all that is evil and clinging to what is good. Thank God with your labors, studying and building and teaching for His honor. Thank Him in everything and for everything!

From Grace to Gratitude

As a youth blessed to grow up in a Reformed church, I was schooled for several years in the lessons of the Heidelberg Catechism. This Reformation confession superbly captures the central tenets of the Christian faith. One of the catechism's memorable features is its three-part structure, explaining in question 2, "all we need to know to live and die in the joy of our salvation" under the three themes of "Our Sin and Misery," "Our Salvation," and "Our Thankfulness." We could affix in our memories three simple words as the core subjects of the catechism: *guilt*, *grace*, and *gratitude*.

What the catechism so succinctly states in its teaching reflects the same trajectory we see in the Scriptures. It is the movement from a sinner's deserved condemnation, to God's amazing grace through Christ, to the humble gratitude of the redeemed. For instance, some of Paul's letters are built according to this pattern: "Divine grace and the constant call to thanksgiving in Paul point to an undeserving act that alters one's fundamental orientation and relationship with God."[6] The example par excellence is his letter to the Romans.

Paul's systematic theology in this letter has been dubbed "the Romans Road." Paul takes us on a journey from misery to hope, from guilt to gratitude. Romans shows our need for salvation, how God provides salvation, and then the results of this salvation in our lives. Along this road, the first signpost is Romans 3:23: "All have sinned and fall short of the glory of God." In character and conduct, all humans are displeasing to God, and there is nobody who stands innocent before Him. Following that is the second Roman signpost

---

6. David W. Pao, *Thanksgiving: An Investigation of a Pauline Theme*, New Studies in Biblical Theology 13 (Downers Grove, Ill.: InterVarsity, 2002), 81–82.

at 6:23, delivering more bad news: "The wages of sin is death." Such is the punishment sinners have earned by their sins—not just temporal, but eternal death.

Even so, the Romans Road is not a dead end. The third signpost announces the wondrous words in the second half of 6:23: "But the gift of God is eternal life in Christ Jesus our Lord." Here is the pathway leading to paradise, but only if we pass the checkpoint at Romans 10:9: "If you confess with your mouth the Lord Jesus and believe in your heart that God has raised Him from the dead, you will be saved." It is only by faith in Christ that you can pass through the gates of His kingdom.

And where does this leave a redeemed sinner today? This is the journey of thankfulness that Paul begins charting in Romans 12:1: "I beseech you therefore, brethren, by the mercies of God, that you present your bodies a living sacrifice, holy, acceptable to God, which is your reasonable service." The "therefore" of 12:1 looks back on the first eleven chapters: first guilt, then grace, now gratitude. The signposts of the Romans Road are inseparably linked. If we are to live as sacrifices, we must know the reason for our sacrifice.

Throughout Scripture, this is the sure pattern for the conduct of God's children: you have been shown amazing grace, so live in humble gratitude to the triune God! Centuries ago, Samuel exhorted the Israelites: "Only fear the LORD, and serve Him in truth with all your heart; for consider what great things He has done for you" (1 Sam. 12:24). By setting our mind on the glories of Christ and considering the great things He has done, God will surely work in us an increase in gratitude.

Reflect . . .

◆ Think back to an earlier question: What do you have that you
did not receive?

◆ Have you ever asked, Who am I, O Lord God, that you have
brought me this far?

◆ So, what is the reason that God has been so good to you?

◆ As you think ahead, will you trust that God for Jesus's sake will
freely give all things needed?

◆ And as you receive God's gifts in Christ, how will you live in
gratitude to Him?

CHAPTER 4

Let Me Count the Ways

Years ago, I led monthly devotions at a retirement home in Hamilton, Ontario, Canada. We would gather for an hour of Scripture reading, hymn singing, prayer, and a short-ish meditation. As a seminary student, I was grateful to get experience in bringing messages of encouragement from Scripture. At first I thought I was impressing the residents with my exegetical insights and rhetorical prowess. But I soon realized that what they really came for was the singing. Whenever I finished my talk and announced that it was time to sing, the elderly ladies and gentlemen would shake off their drowsiness, begin to flip through the collection of classic hymns and spiritual songs, and eagerly make their requests. One of the perennial favorites was "Count Your Blessings":

> When upon life's billows you are tempest tossed,
> When you are discouraged, thinking all is lost,
> Count your many blessings, name them one by one,
> And it will surprise you what the Lord has done.

With rare exceptions, we sang it every month. I admit that it was never my favorite. But the residents loved it, and they sang it with all their heart, especially the refrain:

> Count your blessings, name them one by one;
> Count your blessings, see what God has done.[1]

---

1. Johnson Oatman, "Count Your Blessings," in the public domain.

Count Your Blessings

It is true that "count your blessings" is a hackneyed phrase. It's the kind of trite advice that is easy to give to a sad and struggling person. Yet it remains a beneficial activity for every child of God. It is right that we savor God's good gifts in all their innumerable forms.

This grateful spirit was modeled for me by my neighbors in the retirement home. They were all in the twilight of their lives. Many had impaired mobility and were confined to wheelchairs, some were nearly deaf or blind, and not a few were suffering from the mind-emptying onset of dementia. Yet they were grateful to God, and they sang happily of His goodness to them. Talking to them, I learned they were thankful for a comfortable place to live, for nutritious food, for medical care, for the loved ones who came to visit, and for a lifetime of cherished memories. And they thanked the God who had graciously sustained and encouraged them for long decades of life.

Whether we are young or old, struggling or flourishing, here is the challenge: to be truly aware of how God has blessed us and to sincerely thank Him for His goodness and grace. Some of His gifts are notable, and many appear minuscule. But Charles Spurgeon's counsel is wise: "Let us daily praise God for common mercies—common as we frequently call them, and yet so priceless that when deprived of them we are ready to perish."[2] To borrow a phrase from the contemporary gratitude gurus, it is fitting that God's people undertake a daily gratitude inventory. What have I received?

Any account of God's gifts will range widely. It will encompass everything from material objects like my reliable car, to relational blessings like my marriage, to emotional and spiritual endowments like positivity and perseverance, to opportunities for meaningful work and refreshing rest. The number and diversity of the Father's gifts will be astonishing.

In the months during which I worked on this book, I made it a regular practice to ask people what they were thankful for. I had this

---

2. As quoted in Nancy Leigh DeMoss, *Choosing Gratitude: Your Journey to Joy* (Chicago: Moody, 2009), 113.

conversation with many dozens of people. Many of their answers found their way into this and following chapters, so let me thank them for their contributions! Sometimes when I asked the "thankful question," without hesitation a person would answer by quickly rattling off a dozen or more things. Then they would pause and look at me as if to say, "How many more do you want?" There was too much to express.

In fact, I had a formidable challenge when writing this chapter when I reflected on how best to lead a reader through the happy task of naming God's blessings one by one. As much as I wanted to be systematic in this exercise—and as much as it would agree with my character to be comprehensive—I simply couldn't be. God's vast blessings will always exceed our best efforts to count or quantify. There can be no tidy system of taking a gift inventory. Instead, we are overwhelmed by the magnitude of God's blessings.

Even so, we should take stock. Such an exercise serves as a precautionary measure in our daily struggle against ingratitude. It will also impel us to give God the glory and thanks that are His due. As I've said before, thanksgiving should be the sanctified instinct of the Christian life. William Law said it well: "Would you know him who is the greatest saint in the world? It is not he who prays most or fasts most; it is not he who gives most alms, but it is he who is always thankful to God, who receives everything as an instance of God's goodness and has a heart always ready to praise God for it."[3]

I am convinced that no child of God can grow in gratitude without regularly recounting His many gifts. From the seemingly mundane gift of our daily bread to the obviously miraculous gift of adoption into God's family, a believer's life is truly overwhelmed with the bounty of the Lord's goodness. With open eyes and a grateful heart, we begin the never-ending task of counting our blessings. There are countless specimens for thanksgiving, good gifts for which

3. William Law, *A Serious Call to a Devout and Holy Life* (1729; repr., Mineola, N.Y.: Dover, 2013), 172.

we are grateful to God. To heighten our appreciation of some of these blessings, we'll take a closer look at them.

Specimens for Thanksgiving, Part 1
The Beauty of the Earth
Be thankful for where you live. Wherever in this world you reside, all around is the evidence of God's creative power. His majesty and glory are revealed in the physical geography of this earth. For instance, this might be seen in the immensity of mountains, the power of the ocean, or the solitude of the prairie. Most of us don't reside in alpine villas or beach houses, but we all have occasion to see the simple beauty of God's created world, like the sunlight piercing a foggy winter morning, rainfall pounding the earth, and roughhewn trees standing resolute in the backyard, year after year. Like the psalmist says, calling on every corner and every creature of God's creation to glorify Him: "Praise the LORD from the earth" (Ps. 148:7). For the beauty of His earth, we thank God and give glory to Him.

Technology
Technology is God's gift. While I was in the middle of writing this chapter, my PC began flashing the "blue screen of death," sending out its distress signal that something was perilously wrong. After a short visit to an IT specialist from my congregation, my computer came back doing exactly what it was supposed to—and I was thankful. So often we pay little attention to the technology that facilitates the ease and comfort of our life, whether computers and phones, cars and planes and trains, industrial tools, or any other kind. In the beginning, God mandated people to have dominion over the earth (Gen. 1:26), to develop its potential and harness its power. Through technology we enjoy the fruits of many centuries of this work. We are enabled to work more effectively, travel more safely, and live more healthily. Only when these tools break, fail, or crash do we notice how much we actually depend on them. But these technologies are blessings from God, so we thank Him. Thank God for skilled computer technicians too.

A Godly Spouse

If God joins you with a godly husband or wife, you receive another reason for gratitude. Scripture speaks about the gift of a spouse: "He who finds a wife finds a good thing, and obtains favor from the LORD" (Prov. 18:22). I once asked an elderly brother what he was thankful to God for. Without hesitation, he pointed with a smile across the room to his wife: "Her!" They had been married for more than sixty years, and in a beautiful way they still delighted in each other as blessings from God. The struggles in marriage can be significant, but far greater are the gifts we receive. Thank God for your spouse, and while you're at it, tell your spouse why you're thankful for him or her.

Our Nation

We thank God for our nation, for its safety, its opportunities, its freedom, and its structures. If you have spent your life as a resident of a Western nation, you might very well take this gift for granted. As someone who grew up inside the comfortable borders of Canada, I know that I have failed to appreciate God's blessing of a safe and livable nation. It's difficult for me to imagine living in a country not ruled by law and order or where the leaders do not feel a moral obligation to care for its citizens. But I've spoken with people who left a country disabled by unrest, corruption, and lawlessness and who were able to migrate to a place of peace and stability. They might regret having had to leave home, yet they are deeply grateful for their adopted nation. It's striking how they thank God for things like good hospitals, honest police officers and judges, well-maintained roads, generous social support, and personal security. And if we have these good gifts, so should we be thankful. As Moses said to the Israelites before they entered Canaan, "When you have eaten and are full, then you shall bless the LORD your God for the good land which He has given you" (Deut. 8:10).

Friends

Among the people for whom we're thankful are the friends God has given. Think of how Scripture speaks about the blessing of friendship:

"A friend loves at all times, and a brother is born for adversity" (Prov. 17:17). Throughout our lifetime, we can be surrounded by many acquaintances, have numerous social contacts, and enjoy good relations with several dozens of people. Yet it is probably true that most of us will be blessed in our lifetime with only one or two really close friends. These are the friends who understand you, who tolerate your bad moods, who help you to grow in Christ, who stand beside you on the delightful and the difficult days, who love at all times. Thank God for faithful friends.

The Path of Our Life
Have you ever thanked God for how He has guided your life? Such gratitude requires us to pause and reflect on the trajectory that you have been on until this moment. Today we are where we are—and we are *who* we are—because of innumerable events, personal associations, big and small decisions, blessings and tragedies. Who were your parents? What was your health like in your early years? Where were you raised? What friendships did you make in high school? What career path did you decide to follow? Whom did you marry? What significant events stand out in your life? Maybe a childhood illness, a move to a different country, the death of a loved one, a grievous moral failing, the gift of marriage or parenthood, or something else? The course of anyone's life is complicated. Yet looking back, we can thank God for His faithful providence. He has never stopped upholding and guiding us, and He never will: "The LORD will fulfill his purpose for me; your steadfast love, O LORD, endures forever" (Ps. 138:8 ESV). Even in times of suffering, God has been gracious toward us. As one brother in Christ said, recalling the many heartaches of past years, "I'm thankful to God for His answers to my prayers—answers which have always been good and right."

Children
When meeting with young couples who are preparing to marry, I always encourage them not to assume that God will bless their marriage with children. Life is His gift: "Children are a heritage from

the LORD" (Ps. 127:3). And in His goodness, God often does grant a son, a daughter, even a quiverful of sons and daughters. How does a parent begin to express the sheer wonder and joy of having children, together with the pain and worry, the circuitous path of growth, and the never-ending parade of surprises? It's easy to be so deeply immersed in the experience of raising children that a parent has no time to properly thank God, but it should not be this way. A husband and wife who had not received children for the first several years of marriage spoke to me about the amazing delight they had in their newborn. They thanked God sincerely for the gift of a child, as should every parent.

My Body

The only time that I really take any notice of my body is when it isn't functioning like it should. Fewer problems can feel more pressing and life-dominating than a toothache, a sore back, an eye infection, a migraine, stubborn constipation, or ongoing heart palpitations. For many of us, our body almost always does as it was designed to do, with barely any intervention from us. The body is a beautifully complex amalgam of systems, one that allows us to enjoy God's good world. So we thank Him: "Your hands have made me and fashioned me, an intricate unity" (Job 10:8). I am thankful for legs with which to walk and run, eyes for seeing, lungs for breathing, a tongue for tasting, and a digestive tract for handling all the tasty foods that I am allowed to eat. I am grateful to God for blood that clots, a mind that remembers, and a nose that smells. I thank God for my body and how it works.

Work

I thank God for work. Probably most high school students have been told, "Find a job that you love, and you'll never work another day in your life." This well-meaning counsel doesn't really capture the reality of working in a world overrun by the thorns and thistles of sin's curse. Still, it does highlight the value of having a job that is personally rewarding. God gives us talents and strengths, and He also provides the opportunity to use these gifts. Sometimes a person finds a job in which their gifts are well matched with what is required, where their desire to do something is joined with a good amount of capability. Certainly not everyone is hired into their dream job. But whenever we work, we can take satisfaction in a job well done: building a house, selling a product, repairing a car, delivering a sermon, preparing a meal, representing a client. We thank God that we have been able to use our strength and time and skill for a good purpose. We work with gratitude because God accepts our humble labor as service to Him: "Whatever you do, do it heartily, as to the Lord and not to men, knowing that from the Lord you will receive the reward of the inheritance; for you serve the Lord Christ" (Col. 3:23–24).

Another Day

Today the sun rose again on God's green earth. Today you lived and moved. Today God fed you, and He led you. So be grateful for another day that you're alive under God in heaven: "This is the day the LORD has made; we will rejoice and be glad in it" (Ps. 118:24). Thank God for today, and do not worry about tomorrow.

Family

Family life can be complicated. This is nothing new, as seen in the Bible's many stories of messy families. But what a gift from God are godly parents! And how good to have sisters and brothers and to be blessed with aunts and uncles and cousins and to share life with grandparents and parents-in-law. God blesses us in marvelous ways through the bond of those who are connected to us by blood and marriage. It is reassuring to know that these people are always ready to stand by us. They drive us crazy sometimes, but they are our family. And when we have a shared faith in Christ, the bond is eternally strong and doubly beautiful. In His goodness, God allows many believers the opportunity to "[tell] to the generation to come the praises of the LORD, and His strength and His wonderful works that He has done" (Ps. 78:4). It is a special gift when parents and children, grandparents and grandchildren, uncles and nieces, aunts and nephews, may praise and serve the Lord together. Thank God for family.

Medical Technology

Sometimes I think that I would prefer to live in the Middle Ages—something about the era of knights, castles, and chivalry is very appealing. But on reflection, I realize that there is much to appreciate about living in the twenty-first century. This is particularly in relation to things like medical care. I thank God that I can visit the dentist for regular cleanings and for the occasional filling. I thank God that today there are antibiotics to treat infections, vaccinations for many pernicious diseases, reliable medicine for headaches, safe procedures to remove warts and moles and to mend broken bones. Over the years I have met people who, for instance, suffered a broken femur in a car accident or a smashed pelvis or who have had bone cancer or whose baby simply would not come out the "normal" way. In an earlier time—sometimes only a generation ago—many such things would have resulted in certain death or a life-altering disability. The fact is, those romantic Middle Ages weren't that great for human longevity, with their crude amputations, pointless bloodletting, and only the most rudimentary of medicines. But in our time God has blessed us with amazing advances in medical technology. We thank God, who can heal our diseases (Ps. 103:3). Now the very sick face far better prospects of healing, and we can deal safely with some of the uncomfortable medical conditions we face. Good health care, and access to this care, is one of God's good gifts.

Human Creativity

Maybe you'll agree with me when I say that there is nothing like the pleasure of a good book, such as the amusing adventures of *Don Quixote* or the evocative landscapes of Thomas Hardy. Maybe you'll agree that any music composed by J. S. Bach is a blessing from God or that Johnny Cash is great listening. Or perhaps—quite likely, in fact—you have your own tastes in books and music and art. But is it not a gift from God that we are allowed to enjoy such beauty? We read, and we enter new worlds. We listen, and our spirit is calmed, energized, or filled with a sense of longing. We contemplate a public artwork, a painting, a building, and we praise God for how He has gifted people with creativity and vision (see Ex. 35:35). And we thank Him for how we are allowed to share in the fruit of their labors.

Sleep
We spend a substantial portion of our life sleeping. And we need it. Without having read the scientific studies that have been conducted on sleep, we just know that a good night's rest is vital to our well-being—physically, mentally, and spiritually. I know an elderly sister in Christ who has struggled terribly to fall asleep—and to stay asleep—almost every night for the last couple of decades. She naps in fits and starts during the day and then faces another long night of tossing and turning. For some, sleep is a torment, while for many, sleep is God's gift. Somehow those seven or eight hours provide us with a restoration of energy, a reset of mood, an escape from the day's stresses, a fertile atmosphere for new ideas, a sense of peace, and so much more: "I will both lie down in peace, and sleep; for You alone, O LORD, make me dwell in safety" (Ps. 4:8). And when I awake, I am still with you—thank you, God.

Ordinary Gifts
On any given day, we think a lot about our physical well-being. Jesus knows that we need food to live, and we tend to be anxious if we don't receive it in a timely way. For this reason, it is the first of the things that we request for ourselves in the Lord's Prayer. This petition is rooted in God's promise, as Psalm 34:10 says: "The young lions lack and suffer hunger; but those who seek the LORD shall not lack any good thing." God gives what is essential for life, from food to drink, from oxygen to sunlight, from footwear to clothing. At each of these gifts, we can gratefully pause. Take clothing, for example— perhaps a favorite woolly sweater or a pair of sturdy shoes that has accompanied you on countless walks in the woods—thank God for how He has provided these things. "Perfunctory prayers occur when

we don't see God, His creation, and the human secondary causes He has ordained to cultivate, harvest, and bring these blessings to us, i.e., farmers, ranchers, loggers, carpenters, clothing manufacturers, employees in the produce or meat section of the grocery story, chefs, cooks, etc."[4] But when we are thankful for these ordinary gifts and how they have come to us, God is praised. When we acknowledge the Father's goodness in a cup of tea, some chocolate pudding, and our PB&J sandwich, then "every bit of existence, including our eating and drinking, is like an ongoing hymn."[5] Says Paul in 1 Corinthians 10:31, "Whether you eat or drink, or whatever you do, do all to the glory of God."

Other Areas to Explore
Our gratitude inventory is far from finished. Pondering each of these will suggest further areas of gratitude to explore:

- a house—or better, a home
- laughter
- enjoyable activities: running, snorkeling, quilting, painting, fishing, and many more
- education and educators
- a positive outlook on life
- the rhythm of the four seasons
- your dog, canary, cat, hamster, or other endearing companions
- good memories of past blessings

Interlude: Receive Everything with Thanksgiving
We'll always struggle to be thorough in our catalog of blessings. And little wonder, for the earth is "full of the goodness of the LORD" (Ps. 33:5). In 1 Timothy 4:4 (NIV), Paul affirms something similar:

---

4. Gordon Wilson, *A Different Shade of Green: A Biblical Approach to Environmentalism and the Dominion Mandate* (Moscow, Idaho: Canon Press, 2019), 25.
5. DeJong, *Eucharistic Reciprocity*, 241.

"Everything God created is good, and nothing is to be rejected if it is received with thanksgiving."

It's probably obvious that this text is open to misunderstanding. A person might say, "Because marijuana is part of God's good creation, I don't need to reject it." Or, "God made sexual pleasure, so the more I experience it, the more grateful I will be." What does it mean, then, that we may receive every created thing with thanksgiving?

In 1 Timothy, Paul responds to false teachers who were obsessing over myths and old genealogies and arguing about insignificant points of the law. At the same time, they insisted that the body be treated harshly. To be truly holy, you had to deny yourself the basic comforts of life. Countering their harsh approach, Paul affirms that every handiwork of God is good and useful (see Gen. 1:31). There is no need to flatly reject rich food, alcoholic beverages, or sexual pleasure. Post-fall, this world groans because of sin and its consequences. Even so, God's created things remain good and available to enjoy.

The essential condition, however, is that God's gifts must be received "with thanksgiving." We should recognize the One who has provided His gifts, and then we should respond with worship and adoration. Paul underlines this truth in the next verse, saying that all things can be "consecrated by the word of God and prayer" (1 Tim. 4:5 NIV). Even something that is common and ordinary can be received as a precious gift from God. It is sanctified for use by a thankful and prayerful attitude: "Creaturely goods are gifts when they are enjoyed in the right way."[6] If we can say genuine thanks to God for it, then we are not forbidden to enjoy it. Put another way, we have no right to use God's benefits unless we will faithfully proclaim His praise. His multitude of good gifts ought to move us to much gratitude.

Specimens for Thanksgiving, Part 2

When we turn from God's many earthly blessings to ponder the immense riches of salvation through Christ, words fail. It is not an

---

6. James K. A. Smith, *On the Road with Saint Augustine* (Grand Rapids: Brazos, 2019), 100.

exaggeration to say that every theme here contains an infinite measure of blessing from God. His grace is beyond our understanding in its dimensions, and "the love of Christ…passes knowledge" (Eph. 3:19). In countless volumes over the centuries, Christian authors have explored the many facets of redemption. So much of this theology is doxological; it moves us to praise and adore the God of our salvation. As always, His great goodness inspires our gratitude.

Jesus

In an earlier chapter, we marveled at God's ground for giving, Jesus Christ. Only because of Jesus do we have anything good, and only because of Him has God become our gracious Father. It is impossible to separate salvation's many benefits from our great benefactor, the Son of God. And there are profound riches in each aspect of Christ's person and work. We could meditate with gratitude on His divine nature, His incarnation and humanity, His obedient life, His earthly suffering and crucifixion, His death and resurrection, His ascension and heavenly glory. When we are united to Christ by faith, we have the greatest reason to live in ceaseless thanksgiving, for we have the indescribable gift of His salvation. Here, too, there are countless specimens for thanksgiving to consider.

Baptism

I don't remember my baptism. I know that it took place on a Sunday, way back in March 1978 in a modest church building in Cloverdale, British Columbia, Canada, and that I was wearing an adorable white gown. I don't remember it because I was only a couple of weeks old at the time, and I had no input into whether I should be baptized. My parents presented me for baptism because of the Reformed conviction that God has made a covenant of love with believers and their children and that children should therefore receive the sign and seal of this covenant in baptism. With the sprinkling of a few drops of water on my little forehead, God signified the washing away of my sins with Christ's blood. It was a simple ritual that was quickly done, but God's promises are steadfast. On that day, the triune God publicly vowed that He was willing to be my God and to make me His child. Having given so much, God calls me to faith and to the obedience that comes from faith. As I live in covenant with God, I know that this remains true: "He remembers His covenant forever, the word which He commanded, for a thousand generations" (Ps. 105:8). I thank God for my baptism.

Prayer
Some gifts are beautiful in their simplicity. Consider prayer: it doesn't have to be eloquent, lengthy, or according to a set pattern; it can be a simple and genuine calling on the name of the Lord. Consider how David prays in Psalm 86:4: "To You, O Lord, I lift up my soul." At any time, from any place, in any condition we are privileged to lift up our souls to the living God. Coming to the Father's door, we're allowed to knock and see it opened every time. In Jesus's blood we may draw near. Prayer is a delightful picture of our reconciled relationship with God, for where there used to be animosity and a looming condemnation, through Jesus there is now friendship between us and God. The heart of prayer isn't about *what* we get; it's about *who* we get— God, plus the warmth of His love and fellowship. Thank God for prayer, and then pray without ceasing.

Providence
God's providence is one of the most comforting doctrines of our faith. Talk to a believer who has walked a journey of trouble or sadness, and he might say, "It's the providence of God that carries me—no matter what happens, I know I can trust in Him." Without God's providence, we're just helpless souls floating in a cosmos of uncertainty. But God created the entire universe with the word of His mouth, and He maintains it with the same. Everything is under His control: governments and nations, seasons and disasters, planets and stars, war and peace. The doctrine of God's providence is immense—even infinite in scope—yet it includes the smallest details of our ordinary lives. Perhaps more than through any other way, God wants His glory displayed through His care for His people.

So His fatherly hand is always on us, guiding, giving, shaping, and protecting us. We can be confident, for in His providence there is nothing that "shall be able to separate us from the love of God which is in Christ Jesus our Lord" (Rom. 8:39). When I think about my security in the providence of God, I am grateful.

Freedom to Worship
There are many Christians around the globe who suffer under oppressive political regimes. They must think carefully about how to exercise their faith, lest they be imprisoned or fined. So give thanks to God if you have the freedom to worship publicly. Thank Him if you are allowed to possess the Scriptures and to speak openly about them. Give thanks for the privilege of assembling with fellow believers every Sunday without fear and without hindrance. Be grateful for the protections that are afforded to Christians, such "that we may lead a quiet and peaceable life in all godliness and reverence" (1 Tim. 2:2). Thank the Lord for the freedoms you have received. And remember to pray for those believers who do not have them.

Repentance
My simple question "What are you thankful for?" moved one brother to give an account of how God had brought him to repentance after living in sin for years. It was a sad story of descending into alcoholism and drug addiction, getting into trouble with the law, and shattering almost every relationship in his immediate family and his congregation. But God graciously worked a change of heart. This brother finally started to fight against his sin and then to repair its effects: "I thank God for saving me from myself, for pursuing me when I was running away from Him." Perhaps you haven't had a period when you lived in outright defiance of the Lord, so maybe the contrast between living according to the sinful flesh and walking in the Spirit is less stark for you. But all sinners must repent from their sin and come to God for grace. For "if we confess our sins, He is faithful and just to forgive us our sins and to cleanse us from all unrighteousness" (1 John 1:9). It's only through God's work that we

will ever seek Him and depart from evil. So thank God for the grace of repentance.

Church Family

It is good to belong to a church community. Where else can you experience the joy of the bond of believers, as people of diverse backgrounds, opinions, strengths, and weaknesses are brought together as a family? We call each other brother and sister, and we mean it, for God the Father has made us one in His Son. So we care for each other with prayers and casseroles and birthday cards. We are allowed to share our hardest struggles together and walk beside each other throughout our earthly pilgrimage. We laugh together, we worship together, we play volleyball together, and we spread the gospel together, trying to overlook whatever earthly reasons we might have to ignore or judge each other. If you've been part of a living church community, then you know a little of what David means in Psalm 16:3: "As for the saints who are on the earth, 'They are the excellent ones, in whom is all my delight.'"

The Bible

The Bible is a gift that is at once ordinary and extraordinary. For some Christians, the Bible is so common that we might have a dozen or more copies: one on the nightstand, one near the kitchen table, one slowly discoloring on the car's back seat. To us the Bible is so ordinary that old copies get used as decoration or are simply thrown out. Flipping through its pages feels natural, yet we might forget how explosive this book really is. The Lord says in Jeremiah 23:29, "Is not My word like a fire…and like a hammer that breaks the rock in pieces?" For good reason this book has been at the heart of so much controversy, worship, delight, and transformation. The Bible contains the very mind of God, the true state of humankind, the way of salvation, and the happiness of believers. It is food to nurture and comfort to cheer. It is the traveler's map, the pilgrim's staff, the pilot's compass, the soldier's sword, and the Christian's charter. It is a storehouse of treasure and a river of life. It is a lamp to our feet and a light on our path. Its doctrines are holy, its precepts binding, its histories true, and its wisdom unchangeable. Without the Scriptures we would be utterly lost. Thank God for the Bible and for the privilege of reading it every day.

Faith

I'm thankful that I believe in God. Scripture tells me what God has said about Himself and about who I am and how our relationship can be restored through Jesus. And somehow, I am confident that it's all true. Faith itself defies understanding, for Hebrews 11:1 says that it's "the evidence of things not seen." I accept the existence and nearness of the invisible God. I don't see Him, but I know that I come into God's presence whenever I pray and worship. I don't see Him, but I love Him and want to serve Him. There are many invisible truths whose reality I simply accept by faith: the angels who God sends to protect me, King Jesus ruling from His throne, and heaven as the dwelling place of God together with all those He has already called to Himself. Without faith, almost everything Scripture says would be silliness to me. Without faith, I would not be saved. And apart from God's grace, I would never have faith living within me. So thank God that "it has been granted on behalf of Christ…to believe in Him" (Phil. 1:29).

Our Blessed Hope

Can you be thankful for something promised but not yet received? You can if you know that the promiser is trustworthy. God has vowed that He will one day conquer all His and our enemies, that we will dwell with Him with renewed bodies and souls, and that we will forever enjoy perfect peace. Scripture says,

> Eye has not seen, nor ear heard,
> Nor have entered into the heart of man
> The things which God has prepared for those who
>   love Him. (1 Cor. 2:9)

Heavenly glory is far beyond our earthly understanding, and *everlasting* is too big for our small minds. Yet because God has promised, we are confident. If you're looking forward to this inheritance, you can be at rest. Whatever else might happen in this life, your great enemy Satan will be defeated. Whatever else might happen in this world, your mighty Savior will return in glory. Whether troubles or joys await us tomorrow, soon you'll be blessed beyond measure. When we come to the end of our story, we'll see that there really is no end after all, but life that is everlasting. Thank God for our blessed hope.

Preaching

In His wisdom, God has made powerful the preaching of the gospel. When His word is faithfully expounded, preaching can not only call sinners to Christ but instill true faith in Him as Savior. And God is pleased to nourish our faith for the rest of our lives by that same preaching. The man in the pulpit is a sinner himself, weak and flawed, yet by his stammering words, he brings immense blessing to Christ's people. The preacher's task is wonderful, and his message is glorious: "How beautiful are the feet of those who preach the gospel of peace, who bring glad tidings of good things!" (Rom. 10:15). As a minister of the gospel, I thank God for the great privilege of preaching. But more than this, I thank God for how He has used preaching to draw me to Christ, to increase my love for Him, and to shape my life for Him.

Election

Election is a gift shrouded in mystery, yet by it God makes a display of His great glory. The God who created all things so perfectly in the beginning, the God against whom a rebellion was launched by those who bore His image—this God, instead of destroying His world, chose to save a certain number of undeserving people at His own expense. Election, says Ephesians 1:6, is "to the praise of the glory of His grace, by which He made us accepted in the Beloved." When I asked my gratitude question, someone straightforwardly described the main reason for her gratitude: "That He chose *me*." Thank God for His choice.

Forgiveness

We cannot imagine how often we've sinned. Neither can we imagine the penalty that our sin deserves. Our awareness of sin and its penalty are always partial; therefore, our appreciation for God's forgiving mercy is always incomplete. But the gospel is clear: in Christ we have the complete forgiveness of all our sins. Micah announced this saving message:

> [God] will again have compassion on us,
> And will subdue our iniquities.
>
> You will cast all our sins
> Into the depths of the sea. (7:19)

Because of Christ, God holds no grudges, reopens no wounds, dwells on no past mistakes. When we ask God in repentance and faith, He forgives completely. Every one of our sins is pardoned, and we are declared righteous through faith in Christ. This is life-restoring and life-changing mercy. Thank God!

The Holy Spirit

Like many of God's blessings, the Holy Spirit is a gift who keeps on giving. When a person has the Spirit, she gets to see the glory of Christ the Savior, to trust and to worship Him. When a person has the Spirit, he becomes eager to tell others about his hope. When a person has the Spirit, she hates sin and pursues holiness. It's no wonder that Jesus tells us to ask for this good gift, for the Holy Spirit brings life: "If you then, being evil, know how to give good gifts to your children, how much more will your heavenly Father give the Holy Spirit to those who ask Him!" (Luke 11:13). Whenever we pray, we're not wrenching gifts from the hands of an unwilling master but approaching a loving Father. So we ask the Father for the gift of the Spirit, and then we stand amazed and grateful as He slowly conforms us to the image of God the Son.

God

Sometimes our gratitude is shortsighted. We thank God for only the most immediate things, whatever good gifts we can see and touch at

that moment. But underlying every blessing is God Himself. Funda-
mentally, it is because of *who God is* that we have life, salvation, and
hope. Therefore, we simply and sincerely thank God for His perfections as God, praising Him for the glory of His attributes. Thank God
for His patience. Thank Him for His eternity. Thank God for being
gracious. Thank God that you know Him to be immutable, just, wise,
and sovereign. "Do you see that there is nothing God could ever do
for you or give to you greater than the gift of Himself? If we cannot
be grateful servants of Him who is everything and in whom we have
everything, what *will* make us grateful?"[7] Even when His gifts seem
few, even when hope feels faint or prayer is hard, God is God. In
Christ, He is *our* God, and we thank Him.

Other Areas to Explore
We've looked at another collection of specimens for thanksgiving,
particularly the gifts that relate to God's gracious work of saving
sinners through His Son Jesus Christ. Once again, our gratitude
inventory can keep going for a long time:

- Lord's Supper
- your adoption as God's child
- faithful church leaders
- opportunities to share your faith
- one day for rest and worship every week
- psalms and hymns
- the creeds and confessions of the church

Nothing but Beggars
Our uncomprehensive gratitude inventory has taken us from our
humdrum bowl of oatmeal to grand notions of religious freedom,
to the sacred Scriptures, to the gift of health care, to the mysterious
work of the Holy Spirit, and to precious bonds of marriage, friendship, and the communion of saints. And we're far from done.

---

7. Whitney, *Spiritual Disciplines for the Christian Life*, 113; emphasis original.

All this reminds us of the question with which this book began: "What do you have that you did not receive?" (1 Cor. 4:7). When you look at your life, what is *not* a gift? And once again, G. K. Chesterton describes our status incisively: "Briefly, any person, in any position, is a beggar who has nothing but thanks to give for a service."[8]

With so many gifts for which to be grateful, the activity of thanking God is never completed. But out of love for the triune God, we begin and continue this task. One of the fundamental ways by which we thank Him is through prayer. In the next chapter, we'll explore the response of grateful prayer, but here I share a Puritan prayer that captures well the breadth and depth of God's gifts toward us:

> I bless thee for the soul thou hast created,
>   for adorning it, sanctifying it,
>   though it is fixed in barren soil;
>   for the body thou hast given me,
>   for preserving its strength and vigour,
>   for providing senses to enjoy delights,
>   for the ease and freedom of my limbs,
>   for hands, eyes, ears that do thy bidding;
>   for thy royal bounty providing my daily support,
>   for a full table and overflowing cup,
>   for appetite, taste, sweetness,
>   for social joys of relatives and friends,
>   for ability to serve others,
>   for a heart that feels sorrows and necessities,
>   for a mind to care for my fellow-men,
>   for opportunities of spreading happiness around,
>   for loved ones in the joys of heaven,
>   for my own expectation of seeing thee clearly.
> I love thee above the powers of language to express,
>   for what thou art to thy creatures.
> Increase my love, O my God, through time and eternity.[9]

---

8. G. K. Chesterton, "What Is a Beggar," in *Collected Works* (San Francisco: Ignatius Press, 1988), 29:44.

9. Arthur Bennett, ed., *The Valley of Vision: A Collection of Puritan Prayers and Devotions* (Edinburgh: Banner of Truth, 1975), 15.

If I may be permitted to adapt a line from the sonnet by Eliza-
beth Barrett Browning, "How has God loved me? Let me count the
ways." The ways are so many and various.

Reflect...

 ◆ Have you counted God's blessings to you today?

 ◆ Have you named them one by one?

 ◆ Have you seen what God has done in the significant and small
   events of your life?

 ◆ And have you humbly thanked Him?

CHAPTER 5

A Grateful Heart and Life

Recall a time when you received the surprise of a wonderful gift or an overwhelming act of kindness. In return, what could you say or do? You might have discovered that sometimes there is nothing to do but say thank you. We say it once, then a dozen times. We shake the giver's hand or offer a hug, send a card or a text message. We might bring it up again later just so she doesn't forget how thankful we are.

Consider again our position and privilege. We were desperately low because of our sins—bound for eternal torment—but were lifted up by God's grace in Christ and welcomed into His holy presence forever. No doubt the previous chapter could have been much longer. Our gratitude inventory could have filled many more pages.

For people like us, thanksgiving is the only fitting response. We should speak of our gratitude once, then a thousand times, mentioning our appreciation every day in prayer: "Father, I give You thanks for Your sovereign mercy in Jesus Christ, for what You've done in Him." We never tire of saying it: "Thanks be to You, O God, for Your indescribable gift!" (see 2 Cor. 9:15).

A Grateful Heart

If you've received a good gift today, then be sure that you have thanked God. As John Calvin puts it, "In giving thanks, we celebrate with due praise his benefits toward us, and credit to his generosity every good

that comes to us."[1] This is what David did when he received Israel's
gifts for building the temple at Jerusalem. The tribes were generous
in giving, but David recognized that all these offerings flowed first
from God:

> Now therefore, our God,
> We thank You
> And praise Your glorious name. (1 Chron. 29:13)

Remember how often God instructs His people to thank and
praise Him. For instance, there is the frequent call in the Old Testament to "give thanks to the LORD!" (Ps. 105:1). And there is the
New Testament principle of "giving thanks always for all things to
God the Father in the name of our Lord Jesus Christ" (Eph. 5:20).
Together, these words promote gratitude as an attitude and activity
that should be basic for every believer.

Once more, we should keep our thanksgiving in the right perspective. There is nothing we can give to God in return: "Who has
first given to Him and it shall be repaid to him?" (Rom. 11:35). God
knows this, yet He commands gratitude. In fact, He makes thankfulness the trademark of a Christian. So it is right that we take on our
lips the prayer of the English poet George Herbert:

> Thou that hast giv'n so much to me,
> Give one thing more—a gratefull heart.[2]

Herbert's prayer is apt. He not only acknowledges God's rich generosity, but he also confesses our need for help in thanksgiving. We
pray for a heart that is ready to give God the worship He is worthy
to receive. And as God always does, He gives what He commands. If
we want to grow in the activity of thanking God, Psalm 92:1 assures

---

1. John Calvin, *Institutes of the Christian Religion*, ed. John T. McNeill, trans.
Ford Lewis Battles (Philadelphia: Westminster, 1960), 3.20.28.

2. George Herbert, "Gratefulnesse," in *Herbert*, ed. Dudley Fitts (New York:
Dell Publishing, 1962), 124.

us, "It is good to give thanks to the LORD, and to sing praises to Your name, O Most High."

In this chapter we'll see that the frequent command to give thanks is worked out in patterns of song, prayer, sacrifice, generosity, obedience, and love. An attitude and life of gratitude expresses to God our humble dependence and committed love.

Thankful Prayers

When Psalm 105:1 urges us to "give thanks to the LORD," it also recommends ways in which we may do so. For instance, the next phrase says, "Call upon His name." Calling on God in prayer, we acknowledge how He has provided so many benefits. In prayer, we lift up His name with adoration.

Words can sometimes seem cheap. Compared to all the precious gifts we have received, our passing phrases of gratitude appear a small thing. Yet the Father delights to hear from His grateful children. We see this because the Old Testament contains numerous prayers of thanksgiving. In Jonah 2:9, for example, Jonah acknowledges God's goodness in saving him from the watery deep:

> But I will sacrifice to You
> With the voice of thanksgiving;
> I will pay what I have vowed.

A humble child of God will often speak of his or her gratitude to the Lord.

The prophet Daniel is remembered as a man of prayer. And it is striking that when Scripture describes Daniel's habits of prayer, his praying and his giving thanks are placed in parallel: "He knelt down on his knees three times that day, *and prayed and gave thanks before his God*, as was his custom since early days" (Dan. 6:10). True prayer to God, even in times of severe hardship like Daniel was facing, so often overflows into thanksgiving.

Grateful prayers feature likewise in the New Testament, both in example and in precept. For instance, there are the many places where Paul thanks God for particular gifts, whether granted to him or to his congregations. It is also remarkable how Paul considers thanksgiving to be simultaneous with the Christian's prayer. Even as we make our many requests to the Father or as we seek God's peace amid our anxieties, we should saturate our prayers with gratitude to Him. Consider three passages:

- "Be anxious for nothing, but in everything by prayer and supplication, *with thanksgiving*, let your requests be made known to God" (Phil. 4:6).

- "Continue earnestly in prayer, being vigilant in it *with thanksgiving*" (Col. 4:2).

- "I exhort first of all that supplications, prayers, intercessions, and *giving of thanks* be made for all men" (1 Tim. 2:1).

The New Testament portrays gratitude as a core ingredient for all true prayer. Following this pattern of prayer surely honors God as the good and gracious Father. It is easy to rush through our prayer after breakfast or to launch a dozen urgent requests every evening. But we should remember to thank God for His benefits. With good reason the Heidelberg Catechism in question 116 calls prayer "the most important part of the thankfulness that God requires of us." Having received so much in Christ, His people ought to give thanks profusely.

I recall an old saint whose public prayers were often long strings of thoughtful thank-yous. He thanked God for His forgiving grace, for plentiful food, and for sufficient health. He thanked God for enduring peace, for beloved family and friends, for the soul-restoring Scriptures, for the communion and ministry of the church. Everywhere he looked, he saw God's mercies, and he thanked God for them. Gratitude filled his prayers to the point that someone might have wondered if he would have enough time to make a few requests before rounding it all out with an amen. But a gratitude-filled prayer surely rises like pleasing incense to God (Ps. 141:2).

In praying with thanksgiving, Jesus set a good example for us. When standing at the tomb of Lazarus, about to restore him to life, Jesus first thanks God: "Jesus lifted up His eyes and said, 'Father, I thank You that You have heard Me'" (John 11:41). As He often does during His ministry, Jesus prays. Father and Son were in constant dialogue, and the Father was always responsive to the prayers of His Son. So before Christ asks for anything, He thanks God for always hearing Him.

Prayers of thankfulness are often connected with food, one of God's good gifts. Because there is a long Christian tradition of praying at meals, one finds many examples of saying grace, such as this well-known prayer:

> God is great, and God is good,
> And we thank Him for our food;
> By His hand we all are fed;
> Give us, Lord, our daily bread.

In this also, Jesus modeled gratitude. When Christ prepared to feed the multitude, Matthew reports that He "took the seven loaves and the fish *and gave thanks*, broke them and gave them to His disciples; and the disciples gave to the multitude" (15:36). As a perfectly righteous man—as the second Adam—Jesus did not fail in His gratitude like we all have failed. Rather, He was ever humbly aware of God's good gifts.

When our girls were younger, my wife and I tried to ingrain the need to thank God for their daily bread. No meal could be commenced without offering a prayer of thanksgiving. But this good practice gave rise to curious questions. In the endearing legalism of children, they wanted to know whether to pray for food other than meals. What about this midmorning snack or the doughnut at the coffee shop? Didn't this come from God's hand too? And shouldn't we thank Him for it?

While the tradition of praying at mealtimes is fitting, we should not restrict our thanksgiving prayers to mealtime. When we recognize that everything good is a gift from the good God, we'll also respond to Him with comprehensive and constant thanksgiving. Not just this baloney sandwich is God's blessing but this cappuccino and this morning walk along the lake and this chamber music and this

task for a new day. Once again, G. K. Chesterton prods us to expand
the reach of our gratitude:

> You say grace before meals.
> All right.
> But I say grace before the concert and the opera,
> And grace before the play and pantomime,
> And grace before I open a book,
> And grace before sketching, painting,
> Swimming, fencing, boxing, walking, playing, dancing;
> And grace before I dip the pen in the ink.[3]

Thankful Songs of Worship

Prayers of thanksgiving are often quiet and unseen, but gratitude is
also expressed through communal songs of thanksgiving to God.
Psalm 105 also commends this activity to us. The opening appeal to
God's people, "Oh, give thanks to the LORD!" (v. 1) is elaborated in
verse 2, "Sing to Him, sing psalms to Him." A spirit of thanksgiving
to God will surely generate worshipful singing.

Scripture portrays God's people as a singing people. The saints
lift up their voices in praise because God is glorious and does wondrous things. In Psalm 18, after David has recounted the many works
of the Lord in delivering him from his enemies, he declares, "I will
give thanks to You, O LORD, among the Gentiles, and sing praises to
Your name" (v. 49). The great deeds of the Lord will be the theme of
his happy song.

Singing our thanks to God is also a communal activity. At the
temple, people were dedicated to this public work of thanksgiving.
For instance, 1 Chronicles 16:4 says that David "appointed some of
the Levites to minister before the ark of the LORD, to commemorate,
to thank, and to praise the LORD God of Israel." It's delightful when
worship is spontaneous and unforced, of course. But David recognized that presenting gratitude to God is so essential that he should
appoint personnel for this task. It's not a coincidence that in the same

---

3. Chesterton, "A Grace," in *Collected Works*, 10:43.

chapter, we hear an echo of Scripture's familiar thanksgiving theme; these Levites are designated "to give thanks to the LORD, because His mercy endures forever" (v. 41).

Centuries later, when Nehemiah is leading the reconstruction effort on Jerusalem's walls, he too ensures that God is thanked through praise. He says, "So I brought the leaders of Judah up on the wall, and appointed two large thanksgiving choirs" (Neh. 12:31; see also v. 40). At this special moment in Israel's history, it was right that God be thanked in a fulsome way.

The worship of Psalm 136 amplifies Scripture's thanksgiving refrain. Verse 1 sets the tone: "Oh, give thanks to the LORD, for He is good! For His mercy endures forever." Throughout the psalm, the people celebrate the goodness and grace of the Lord. Every verse describes a new facet of God's power and incites His people to a response of thanksgiving. The refrain is heard twenty-six times: "for His mercy endures forever." The cumulative effect is to render the worshipers awestruck and humbled. They conclude the praise of Psalm 136 with one more surge of gratitude: "Oh, give thanks to the God of heaven! For His mercy endures forever" (v. 26).

The keynote theme of Scripture and our lives is the great and marvelous works of God. In Christ, God has redeemed us from sin and death. Says John Calvin, "We are well-nigh overwhelmed by so great and so plenteous an outpouring of benefactions, by so many and mighty miracles discerned wherever one looks, that we never lack reason and occasion for praise and thanksgiving."[4] It should be our chorus and refrain each day. Paul writes in Ephesians 5:19–20, "Singing and making melody in your heart to the Lord, *giving thanks always* for all things to God the Father in the name of our Lord Jesus Christ." It is fitting then, that many Reformation liturgies reflect the impulse of gratitude toward God. After hearing the gospel and receiving the full and free pardon of sins, the church responds with thanksgiving that they express in song and prayer.[5]

---

4. Calvin, *Institutes*, 3.20.28.
5. Chapell, *Christ-Centered Worship*, 92.

Even if you can't sing or don't like to sing, give praise to the Lord. Gratefully sing with your family around the dinner table. Sing with your friends. Sing in church. Have a favorite song of praise in your heart during the week: "Deeply felt thankfulness produces a sound from our voices that is robust and enthusiastic."[6] God delights in our adoration when we take a song on our lips with sincere praise: "[Sing] psalms and hymns and spiritual songs, with thankfulness in your hearts to God" (Col. 3:16 ESV).

Thankful Giving

Our thanksgiving is witnessed in our giving. When God, who is the overflowing fountain of all good, generously pours out His gifts, this generosity should overflow from us toward other people. God's blessings cause us to be a blessing. Colossians 2 speaks of how we ought to be "abounding...with thanksgiving" (Col. 2:7), or as the New International Version puts it, "overflowing." If we are overflowing with thankfulness for God's abounding grace, this will be evident.

Our life has a vertical orientation, for we live in loving relationship with God our Creator and Savior. But true gratitude is not one-directional, from earth to heaven. Gratitude also activates us to serve amid our earthly relationships. Being thankful to God should lead us to love and bless the people whom He has placed in our life. Michael Horton says it well: "When we are overwhelmed by the superabundance of God's gracious gift, we express our gratitude in horizontal works of love and service to the neighbor."[7]

Grateful giving is explored in 2 Corinthians 8–9. In the early years of the church, there was a lot of concern for the believers in Jerusalem and Judea. Acts tells about a severe famine that afflicted the Roman Empire, particularly the area of Palestine. So Paul exhorted the Corinthians to show generosity to the poor. He told them, "God is able to make all grace abound toward you, that you, always having

---

6. Keith and Kristyn Getty, *Sing! How Worship Transforms Your Life, Family, and Church* (Nashville, Tenn.: B&H, 2017), 18.

7. Michael Scott Horton, *Ordinary: Sustainable Faith in a Radical, Restless World* (Grand Rapids: Zondervan, 2014), 197.

all sufficiency in all things, may have an abundance for every good work" (2 Cor. 9:8). He highlights that this is why God gives so generously: it is not so that we may merely satisfy our own desires, but so that we may meet the needs of others.

Indeed, God's giving is not meant to be the end of a process. His grace must never stop with us but be passed on. Calvin explains, "Whatever benefits we obtain from the Lord have been entrusted to us on this condition: that they be applied to the common good of the church. And therefore the lawful use of all benefits consists in a liberal and kindly sharing of them with others."[8] If grace is like a sound, it must echo and reecho. If grace is like a stone thrown into a pond, the ripples must keep spreading. God's grace should turn me into a gracious person. My thankfulness to God should make other people thankful for me.

And as Paul reminded the Corinthians, when we cheerfully give, we never end up with less than what we had. God's promise is that when we faithfully give, He will overflow toward us. Proverbs 3 says,

> Honor the LORD with your possessions,
> And with the firstfruits of all your increase;
> So your barns will be filled with plenty,
> And your vats will overflow with new wine. (vv. 9–10)

Even if you don't have barns and vats, God will keep His riches overflowing toward you. A. W. Tozer comments on the richness of giving, "Gratitude is an offering precious in the sight of God, and it is one that the poorest of us can make and be not poorer but richer for having made it."[9]

Interlude: Who Has Given to God?

What do you get for the person who has everything? This is the problem whenever world leaders get together. Say the president of the United States has hosted the prime minister of Canada for a few

---

8. Calvin, *Institutes*, 3.7.5.
9. A. W. Tozer, *The Set of the Sail* (Chicago: Moody, 1986), 132.

days of high-level talks. When the PM leaves, it would be discourte-
ous not to give the president a thank-you gift. But what is a suitable
present for the most powerful person in the world, someone with no
shortage of earthly resources?

We experience a similar problem when thanking God. We ought
to worship God for all He has lavished on us in Christ. But what
worthwhile thing could we ever present? The almighty God doesn't
need our prayers, songs, or financial gifts. So how should we regard
our gratitude to the Lord?

In Psalm 50 Asaph instructs us about the true spirit of thanksgiving. In the psalm's background is the Israelite practice of bringing
a variety of gifts to God at the temple. God wanted these sacrifices,
for He told His people to bring fellowship offerings, sin offerings,
thank offerings, and guilt offerings. And for their part, Israel had
been scrupulous in worship. God says,

> I will not rebuke you for your sacrifices
> Or your burnt offerings,
> Which are continually before Me. (v. 8)

He takes no issue with the outward form of their worship. Today,
we might compare it to our liturgies being carefully fashioned, our
songs well selected, and the offertory collection overflowing.

But something is amiss. The people think that God needed these
sacrifices, that He was eager to see what they brought Him. If the
people impressed Him at the temple, surely He would give success
in the home, on the fields, or at war. Yet how wrong! So the Lord
rebukes His people in Psalm 50. "The Mighty One, God the LORD"
(v. 1) has no need for human worship. He doesn't depend on our
contributions. After all, the bulls and goats that Israel brought were
already His (vv. 10–11). It was all His blessing. To repeat Romans
11:35, "Who has first given to Him and it shall be repaid to him?"

When God's people thank Him, He wants more than first-rate
animals or produce. He also wants more than on-key singing, faithful tithing, or copious prayer. God wants our grateful heart! Think
again of Acts 17:24–25: "God, who made the world and everything

in it, since He is Lord of heaven and earth, does not dwell in temples made with hands. Nor is He worshiped with men's hands, *as though He needed anything*, since He gives to all life, breath, and all things." Any payment to God is inadequate; it is "an asymmetrical return for the gift."[10] God teaches us to view our acts of worship rightly and realistically.

Asaph therefore highlights just one sacrifice as essential: "Offer to God thanksgiving" (Ps. 50:14). Literally, he says, "make a thank offering." According to the law, a thank offering was offered in the context of a believer's gratitude, when a person was grateful for deliverance from enemies or for healing or for some other answered prayer. A thank offering acknowledged to God that you were indebted to His generosity and kindness.

Still today, God seeks a people who are moved by His love and who want to love Him in return. Peter says that our calling is "to offer up spiritual sacrifices acceptable to God through Jesus Christ" (1 Peter 2:5). Humbly acknowledge that you are indebted to His generosity and kindness. You received a gift; you didn't earn it, so you simply want to thank the Lord.

Thanking Other People

If we have thankful spirits, we will grow in the awareness of how God has blessed us with the gift of other people. Here, too, we see the horizontal orientation of gratitude: being thankful to God *for* other people should lead us to be thankful *toward* them. Dietrich Bonhoeffer observes, "In ordinary life we hardly realize that we receive a great deal more than we give, and that it is only with gratitude that life becomes rich. It is very easy to overestimate the importance of our own achievements in comparison with what we owe to others."[11] So it is fitting that a grateful Christian develops a habit of reaching out to thank other people. Perhaps in person, by phone, or through

---

10. DeJong, *Eucharistic Reciprocity*, 204.
11. Dietrich Bonhoeffer, *Letters and Papers from Prison*, ed. Eberhard Bethge (London: SCM, 1953), 109.

email or social media, we let them know that we are grateful for who
they are and what they do.

First, we could show our gratitude to someone who does not
expect it. Perhaps it is the checkout person in the grocery store who
packs your groceries with care. Perhaps it is the stranger on the bus
who gives up her seat for an elderly woman.

Second, we could thank the people who have supported and
helped us. Once again, Paul sets an example of gratitude. In Philippians 4:10–19, he thanks the Philippians for how they looked after
his material needs. In 2 Timothy 1:16–17, he acknowledges how
Onesiphorus searched for him in Rome to bring encouragement.
This requires us to think back: Who has influenced you or cared for
you? Perhaps a high school teacher who had a key role in shaping
your career path. Perhaps parents who were faithful in going to all
your music recitals or sports games, and now you finally appreciate
what a sacrifice that was. Perhaps a friend who stood by you in your
darkest hour. In a spirit of gratitude, it is good to reach out and say
thank you.

Third, it is right that we thank the people in our life who continue to bless us: friends, spouse, parents, brothers and sisters in a
biological family, brothers and sisters in Christ. Relationships can be
messy and difficult. Yet it is often in these struggles that we realize
how God is blessing us through our interaction with others.

This kind of gratitude is a good counterbalance to the envy or
resentment that we sometimes harbor against other people: "Whereas
a resentful person is quick to observe offenses and blame others, a
grateful person is eager to see goodness in others and inclined to
reciprocate with similar kindness."[12]

It also enhances our relationships when we take the time to
reflect on their meaning, value, and health. For instance, a husband
should take a moment or two to consider how his wife is a blessing to
him through her wisdom, reliability, and unflagging support. Hope-
fully he will then be moved to thank the Lord and to value his wife.

---

12. DeJong, *Eucharistic Reciprocity*, 227.

Or a church member should reflect on the many blessings of belonging to the body of Christ in a particular place. She might then be less inclined to complain about or criticize her fellow members, but instead she will thank Christ for including her and then serve others with joy. The examples can be multiplied: whenever we treasure the gift of a relationship and thank God for it, we should consider how we can give back.

For whom in your life do you thank God? Have you thanked God for them? And have you told them that you are thankful?

Thankful Living

Is our gratitude like the icing on a cupcake or like the mashed banana in a slice of banana bread? We might think of gratitude as the topping on our day: a thankful evening prayer, a glad song of worship after the sermon, a thank-you card, an appreciative word to our neighbor. Such things are like a layer of sweet icing added after everything else. But gratitude should be more like the banana that permeates your favorite loaf, mixed and commingled with all the other ingredients. Gratitude isn't the final layer on a life of blessing; it is basic to our life, part of its very flavor and color.

Consider how Scripture intertwines thanksgiving into the entire Christian life: "And *whatever you do* in word or deed, do all in the name of the Lord Jesus, giving thanks to God the Father through Him" (Col. 3:17). In everything we say or do, it should be evident that we are grateful to God. Acknowledging that Christ has given all, we seek to give all. Likewise, 1 Thessalonians 5:18 exhorts us, "*in everything* give thanks." The word *everything* is inescapably comprehensive. God requires a gratitude that touches all aspects of our existence, a gratitude that is expressed in a life of good works.

Over the centuries, there has been a lot of debate over the place of good works in the Christian life. Does our obedience to God's law earn us any merit in His judgment? Or should we generally avoid any talk of rule-keeping to preserve the teaching that salvation is by grace alone? The legalist tendencies of some Christians have led others to abandon the notion of good works. Yet Scripture teaches that our good works are properly motivated by our gratitude to the Lord. Obedience is a loving response to God for His sovereign grace. It has been rightly said, "Love is the child of gratitude. Love grows as gratitude is felt and then breaks out into praise and thanksgiving to God."[13]

In the glad recognition of our indebtedness to God, thankfulness is the one true motive for Christian living. When we have considered the full weight of our sin and misery and admired salvation's beauty, we present the only possible response: thanksgiving. It should become like the very breath in our lungs: gratitude.

The Heidelberg Catechism reflects the movement from grace to gratitude by explaining the Ten Commandments in its third section, "Our Thankfulness." After tracing the trajectory from the misery of human guilt to the glory of God's grace in Christ, in question 86 the catechism asks, "Why must we yet do good works?" Not far in the background is the false teaching of works righteousness rejected by the catechism. It even forms part of the question: "Since we have been delivered from our misery by grace alone through Christ, *without any merit of our own*, why must we yet do good works?" And a key component of the answer is this: "So that with our whole life we may show ourselves *thankful* to God, and He may be praised by us" (emphases added).

Scripture contrasts an obedient and thankful life with the disobedience of ingratitude. In Deuteronomy 32:6 (NIV), Moses admonishes the wayward Israelites; he reminds them of the perversity they have shown to God, their rock and Savior: "Is this the way you repay the LORD, you foolish and unwise people?" After everything God did for His nation, He was worthy of their quiet trust and submission. And the question could be asked about our own willful acts of disobedience, "Is this the way you repay the Lord?"

The sketch of the Christian life in Ephesians 5 shows how sin is incompatible with gratitude. Among the saints there should not be uncleanness, "neither filthiness, nor foolish talking, nor coarse

---

13. Bounds, "Essentials of Prayer," 306.

jesting, which are not fitting, *but rather giving of thanks*" (Eph. 5:4). Notably, a life that is rooted in thanksgiving is the converse of an evil life. All the words and deeds of redeemed sinners should be different because they gratefully recognize God's saving love in Christ.

Persisting in Thanksgiving

Maybe you've experienced how small your gratitude can seem. The greater the gift, the more insignificant gratitude feels. Someone gives you a valuable present, makes a sacrifice for your cause, or even saves your life. In that moment, any words of thanksgiving can seem very small. In human terms, gratitude always puts us in a lower place. And expressing gratitude shows us that we are indebted and dependent. This is exactly our position before God, for He has saved our life in Christ. Our gratitude can seem very small.

When a person gives an obviously humble or lowly gift, we tell ourselves, "It's the thought that counts." We say that about gifts from little children or maybe from ill-informed husbands. It isn't much, or not quite what we hoped for, but a sincere gift means that a person has tried to express his or her love.

For instance, think of the artwork of little children. A child will happily give her artwork to a parent or send a homemade birthday card to Grandma. The child's work really isn't much. By any artistic standard, it is amateur. It is messy and imperfect, but it is received with joy and pleasure. Grandma puts it on the fridge or hangs it on the wall because she knows that this humble gift was given in love.

God doesn't reject our humble and flawed efforts at Christian service; rather, He graciously welcomes them. He takes pleasure in our good works because we are united to Christ and are being conformed to His image. By our will and work, God is honored. He loves our prayers, even if they are short and simple. He delights to hear our singing, even if it's off-key. He finds joy in our service and gifts, even if they don't look remarkable. God receives it for His own glory.

And so we ought to keep thanking Him. We're not done once Thanksgiving Day has come and gone for another year. Neither are we done once we've thanked the Lord for a few things at our mealtime or bedtime prayer. Like the Holy Spirit says, "Give thanks *always!*" If you love what God has done for you in Christ, be devoted to worshiping Him. If you have been blessed materially, be ready to give something back to Him. While you have life and breath, use it to praise the Lord. God desires your gifts, He delights in your thanksgiving, and He treasures the loving spirit from which it overflows.

Reflect . . .

◆ In what practical ways are you showing thanks to God?

◆ How much does gratitude permeate your daily prayers?

◆ Does a spirit of thankfulness sanctify your gifts to the Lord and to others?

◆ Do you love to make a joyful noise to the Lord together with His people?

◆ How can your entire life be an expression of your thanksgiving to God?

CHAPTER 6

Gratitude Undermined

To be thankful does not seem difficult. Without a lot of effort, we can express gratitude to family at the dinner table and to neighbors at the grocery store:

> Thank you.
> *Gracias.*
> *Merci beaucoup.*
> *Ta.*
> *Bedankt.*

We know that when we have been given something, gratitude is the right attitude. In fact, we can't stand it when people are ungrateful. It irks us when people fail to show proper thanks.

Whenever we see ingratitude and feel our anger heating up, we should look in the mirror. Recall that ingratitude is basic to our sinful equipment as fallen humans. This means that it isn't something we are going to easily overcome.

I remember this all too well from my childhood. My parents would treat us kids to a week of holidays in the mountains or take us out for ice cream on Saturday night or ensure that we had enough food to eat and decent clothes to wear. But ingratitude was always lurking. We would complain about the hand-me-down jeans with the patched knee. We would fight in the car on the way to the restaurant. We would be grumpy because the rain and mosquitoes meant that our vacation was not the idyllic paradise we were hoping for. It is embarrassing to think about how unthankful I once was. And regrettably, it isn't something that I've grown out of entirely. For example, when I think about how capably and constantly my dear wife works to take care of our family and reflect on how little I thank her, I am humbled. I still have a lot to learn about being grateful.

If ingratitude to God is near the root of all sin, then it is unsurprising that our thankfulness is easily undermined. Instead of giving God His due, we remain unmoved or indifferent. But as we become more aware of the obstacles to gratitude, we seek to avoid them and to cultivate a steadfast heart of praise.

Does God Notice?

We usually notice when people say thanks to us, and we definitely notice when people do not. Does God notice, then, when we withhold our gratitude? Or when our thanksgiving prayers resemble the casual thanks that we mumble to the attendant at the gas station? And if He does notice, does He merely consider it poor manners, like when kids grab a cookie or candy without saying thanks? Or is it much worse?

Alongside our many other failings, we might consider ingratitude to be insignificant. But, says Jerry Bridges, "It is an affront and insult to the One who created us and sustains us in every second of our lives."[1] God wants a thankful people who delight in His praise. This is certainly not because God is like us, we who are often in need of a boost to our ego. Neither is thankfulness about paying God back for His gifts. Remember Romans 11:35: "Who has first given to Him and it shall be repaid to him?"

Gratitude is our serious and joyful obligation to honor God for His great goodness. He wants people to see who He is and to stand in awe of Him. He is so deserving of this glory that it's an offense when we do not respond to God with praise. God so frequently commands us to give thanks to the Lord probably because He knows that we will often neglect the task of gratitude. God wants all people, and

---

1. Jerry Bridges, *Respectable Sins* (Colorado Springs: NavPress, 2007), 81.

especially His children, to thank Him for His gifts. And yet we'll see in this chapter how we forget to acknowledge God or how we turn His gifts into idols, act entitled to His blessings, take His gifts for granted, or are discontent with what He has given.

Forgetting to Thank God

The reflexive "thank you" is engrained in our patterns of speech. Yet it is all too possible to forget to thank God. Luke recounts a striking story about such forgetfulness. When Jesus passes through a village one day, He meets ten men with leprosy (Luke 17:11–19). In the dire need of their condition, they cry for help, "Jesus, Master, have mercy on us!" (v. 13). And in His compassion-filled response, Jesus sends the ten men to the priest.

As the lepers depart, they are suddenly healed: their skin is transformed from being black and mushy and without feeling to being pink and healthy and alive. The priest can declare them clean and restore them to the communion of God's people. For the lepers, this was more than a marvelous restoration of health; it was a life-changing encounter, unexpected and undeserved. But only one of the lepers, a Samaritan, returns. Coming to Jesus, he "fell down on his face at His feet, giving Him thanks" (v. 16).

Jesus makes explicit what must have been on the mind of everyone present: "Were there not ten cleansed? But where are the nine?" (v. 17). We don't know. Maybe one went to celebrate—there was a lot of living to catch up on. Maybe another was too shy to approach the Master amid all His followers. Another might have been too proud. Perhaps one leper was overwhelmed with excitement, or another one couldn't find Jesus when he came back. Wherever the other men were, only one remembered to thank the Lord.

This failure to give thanks is captured in an imaginative poem, "But Where Are the Nine?" It is marked by the regretful refrain, "I meant to go back—oh, I meant to go back!"[2] Even if the others

---

2. Author unknown, "But Where Are the Nine?," in *Knight's Treasury of Illustrations*, ed. Walter B. Knight (Grand Rapids: Eerdmans, 1963), 404.

had good intentions to thank Him, only one acknowledged Jesus. He bowed and praised Christ as the life-giving Lord: "The joy that exceeded the priest's pronouncement that he was clean was the joy of his heart being full of love for Jesus Christ."[3]

When we read this story, we are shocked by the ingratitude of the nine men. After being so blessed, couldn't they have offered a single word of thanks to Jesus? Yet surely each of us is guilty of the same ingratitude. We forget to thank God for His good gifts. We receive much yet say little.

To where does our gratitude disappear? Perhaps it is swallowed up in the happy moments of enjoying God's gift. Perhaps we have good intentions to say thank you later, when we do our evening prayers or when we attend church next Sunday: "I meant to go back—oh, I meant to go back!" Perhaps we are proud and resent being perceived as needy once again. Perhaps we simply forget because our mind is frail and our spirit is weak.

However we try to excuse our failure to be thankful, it is more than a cognitive deficiency: "Ingratitude and forgetfulness are ultimately moral rather than mental; they are the direct expression of sin."[4] Forgetfulness can be countered only by remembrance. And remembrance requires effort. Bridges asks us, "Have you stopped today to give thanks to God for delivering you from the domain of darkness and transferring you to the kingdom of His Son?"[5]

We should yearn to live in the spirit of the healed leper. In thankfulness we gladly bow before our Lord for saving us from bondage to death and decay. Like the healed lepers, we have new life because of what Christ has done for us. Redeemed by grace, we resolve to give constant praise to the Lord.

---

3. James W. Beeke and Joel R. Beeke, *Developing a Healthy Prayer Life* (Grand Rapids: Reformation Heritage Books, 2010), 34.

4. Guinness, *The Call*, 260.

5. Bridges, *Respectable Sins*, 80.

Turning God's Gifts into Idols

Every one of God's gifts presents both an opportunity and a challenge. His blessings afford us the opportunity to serve for His glory and our neighbor's benefit. But because of our sinfulness, God's blessings also arouse the temptation to idolatry. We have a deep-seated preference for what is physical, visible, and earthly. This leads us to turn God's gifts against Him, idolizing the good things He has given. For instance, God gives more than sufficient money, and we begin to trust in our financial assets. God gives a godly husband, and we find security in his physical or emotional strength. God gives a vocational skill such as computer programming or animal husbandry or teaching, and we come to build our identity on productivity and competence.

We saw in Romans 1 how ingratitude is basic to our fallen condition. It is our native bent to worship and serve the creature rather than the Creator (see Rom. 1:25). As Michael Horton observes,

> At its heart sin is the eclipse of thankfulness toward God (Rom. 1:21). Why thankfulness? Because rather than seeing ourselves as self-creators who choose our own identity and purpose, the biblical worldview tells us that we are on the receiving end of our existence. We are beholden to someone else. Our life is a gift from God, not our own achievement. And our ingratitude is the clearest expression that we have idolized ourselves.[6]

Unbelieving humankind refuses to recognize God as the Giver. A hardened heart cannot give thanks to the Lord. Consequently, Scripture says that this will typify the wickedness in the last days: people will be "unthankful" (2 Tim. 3:2).

Our tendency to idolatry reveals the need for regular self-examination. As I receive God's good gifts in their many varieties, am I tempted to idolize them? Do I find security in my material things? Do I regard my loved ones as more precious than God? Do I get more pleasure from earthly experiences than from enjoying

---

6. Horton, *Ordinary*, 89.

fellowship with Christ? In this connection, our prayers of thanks-giving can be revealing: "The unvarnished truth is that what we most frequently give thanks for betrays what we most highly value."[7] Do we delight in the gifts, or do we delight in the Giver? In what have we placed our trust?

Idolatry's surest remedy is learning to delight in the triune God. Knowing the Father through His Son and Spirit, we see that He is worthy of wholehearted trust and obedience. God in heaven is good and gracious, the overflowing fountain of blessing, the only source of truth and life. And so we should come to expect our security and meaning not in any earthly thing but in the Lord alone: "Thanksgiv-ing by its very nature is anti-idol polemic."[8] Seeing God as the Giver and worshiping Him, we appreciate but do not idolize His gifts. Says James K. A. Smith, "It's when I stop overexpecting from creation that it becomes something I can hold with an open hand, lightly but gratefully."[9]

Acting Entitled

"I am entitled to my entitlements." So said a Canadian politician some years ago. He had been asked why he should still receive a monetary severance package after resigning from a government cor-poration under a cloud of scandal. Legally he was right, but his answer grated on many people. We don't like the notion of entitlement, that a person inherently deserves privileges or special treatment.

In the time of Jesus, many of the religious elite believed they were entitled to God's blessings by virtue of being observant Jews. John the Baptist warned them, "Do not think to say to yourselves, 'We have Abraham as our father'" (Matt. 3:9). These same leaders took prestigious places at dinners and in the synagogues (Matt. 23:6), craved public attention and titles of honor (v. 7), and loved

---

7. D. A. Carson, *Praying with Paul: A Call to Spiritual Reformation*, 2nd ed. (Grand Rapids: Baker Academic, 2014), 23.

8. Pao, *Thanksgiving: An Investigation of a Pauline Theme*, 97.

9. Smith, *On the Road with Saint Augustine*, 100.

receiving praise for their strict adherence to the law (v. 5). In short, they thought they deserved all they received.

Entitlement culture is endemic in this world, not just among the elite. It's because the attitude of entitlement is instinctive to all our hearts. I want the good things of life—happiness, recognition, money, leisure, health, acceptance—and I think that I deserve them. If I don't receive these things or they are not quite to my liking or they are not as good or plentiful as my neighbor's, I will complain. From birth we are zealous for what is ours: "The claim from our earliest years that something 'is mine' is a manifestation of fallen human nature."[10] And the lamentable result of our sense of entitlement is that we won't be grateful for God's blessings. We are nonchalant about them because God *owes* us.

The alternative, of course, is the quiet appreciation of a beggar who has been granted whatever precious gift he needed. Because he didn't earn it and cannot repay it, he is deeply grateful, and in his gratitude there is delight. It is the delight of receiving, the pleasure of being released from the economy of merit. It is the joy of having no obligation but to express sincere thanksgiving. Paul David Tripp puts it well:

> The DNA of joy is gratitude. When I am living in self-focused, demanding entitlement, I will find it very hard to be joyful. I will find endless reasons to complain. But if I am living in awe of God's existence, sovereignty, and grace, coupled with a knowledge of the depth of my own need, I will find reasons to be thankful all around me. And as I do, I will live with the constant joy of gratitude.[11]

When we look at our life with grace-colored glasses, we will acknowledge what we deserve (nothing) and appreciate what we have actually received (everything). It's all grace. This increases our

---

10. Frank S. Alexander, "Property and Christian Theology," in *Christianity and Law: An Introduction*, ed. John Witte Jr. and Frank S. Alexander (Cambridge: Cambridge University Press, 2008), 206.

11. Paul David Tripp, *Awe: Why It Matters for Everything We Think, Say, and Do* (Wheaton, Ill.: Crossway, 2015), 128.

gratitude for the good gifts of our gracious Father. In this spirit, G. K. Chesterton pronounced a memorable beatitude: "Blessed is he who expecteth nothing, for he shall enjoy everything."[12]

Taking It for Granted

If you've had the thrill of getting a new and shiny possession, then you'll also know how quickly the excitement can wane. The enthusiastic unboxing of your new iPhone becomes the frustration of yet another software update. The new car smell in your Ford fades. Even the person we once fell in love with begins to look a little tired. The magic of the new wears off, and soon we're taking God's good gifts for granted. Even though we prayerfully asked for His blessings and happily received them, perhaps we quietly assumed that we were going to get them anyway.

The Israelites showed how hard it can be to value God's gifts rightly. God had delivered them from Egyptian captivity, opened the sea for them to pass through, and was now leading them through the desert. They had a spring in their step and a song on their lips as they went forth. Yet as the trip entered its second month, the fuel gauge was getting perilously close to empty. Stomachs were rumbling, and mouths were getting dry and parched.

How did God's people respond? With murmuring. They remembered how in the good old days along the Nile, the food supply was so much better. Facing the cruel uncertainty of the desert, they complained against God. And this was a serious failing: "For as thankfulness is an express acknowledgement of the goodness of God towards you, so repinings and complaints are as plain accusations of God's want of goodness towards you."[13]

Yet God was gracious. He hushed their grumbling with His promise: "I will rain bread from heaven for you" (Ex. 16:4). With manna God would feed them every day until their arrival at Canaan. But then the Israelites even started to complain about the marvelous

---

12. Chesterton, *St. Francis of Assisi*, 75.
13. Law, *Serious Call to a Devout and Holy Life, 172.*

manna. It was a stunning miracle that God could feed so many thousands—day after day, so freely, so fully, so faithfully. Yet God's people tired of the miracle and came to resent its predictability. The Israelites griped that the manna wasn't meat; they longed for leeks and grumbled for garlic. Indeed, "resentment and gratitude cannot coexist, since resentment blocks the perception and experience of life as a gift."[14] As obvious and beautiful as it was, they could no longer see God's goodness.

It's a familiar pattern, for we are hardly better than the Israelites. Soon after receiving a blessing, we stop appreciating it. Psychologists refer to this as *habituation*, the tendency to quickly adjust to new circumstances and become accustomed to our changed reality. Says Pink, "Gratitude is the return justly required from the objects of his beneficence; yet it is often withheld from our great Benefactor simply because his goodness is so constant and so abundant."[15] Like the Israelites, we might even find fault with God's blessings, wishing our security was a little more secure, our happiness was a little happier.

But the good God wants His people to acknowledge Him. In Exodus, God commands that a jar of manna "be kept for your generations, that they may see the bread with which I fed you in the wilderness" (Ex. 16:32). The jar was to be a constant reminder of how God provided for the Israelites in the desert, a prompt to thank and praise Him for His ongoing care.

We should celebrate the Lord's daily mercies in a similar way. What has God given you today? Did your car start this morning? Today have you enjoyed food and drink? Could you rest? Could you work? Do you have people around whom you love and who love you? Counting God's daily blessings is something like having a jar of manna. We should mentally store up one gift from God, and another, and another, and one more—and soon the jar is full to overflowing and we are moved to thank the Lord.

14. Nouwen, *Return of the Prodigal Son*, 85.
15. Pink, *Attributes of God*, 77.

THANK GOD

This is a good place to reprise the quotation from earlier: "When it comes to life, the critical thing is whether you take things for granted or take them with gratitude." What's in your jar of manna?

Taking the Credit

Few things kill gratitude as quickly as pride. Surveying our many possessions or our high position, we harbor the thought that we've earned these things ourselves. "As Bart Simpson, America's favorite cartoon kid, put it baldly when asked to say grace at supper time, 'Dear God, we pay for all this ourselves. So thanks for nothing.'"[16] Of course, we would never actually pray in this manner, but just below the surface of our prayer this proud attitude can be skulking.

Once again, the Israelites show how easy it is to take the credit. In Deuteronomy 8, Moses addresses them as they prepare to enter the promised land. Canaan will be a prosperous country, a place of good eating, beautiful houses, thriving herds and flocks, and heaps of silver and gold. But what will happen because of this prosperity? Israel's heart will be lifted up, and they will "forget the LORD [their] God who brought [them] out of the land of Egypt" (Deut. 8:14). So it has always been. In times of blessing, we are tempted to forget God's mercies and to think that it should all be credited to us.

This is sadly ironic, for receiving God's blessings should actually make us acknowledge our weakness and dependence. But Moses is afraid that once they are in the land, the people will say, "My power and the might of my hand have gained me this wealth" (Deut. 8:17). Admiring their strong cities, they will remember how they once had to fight to take them. Weighing their rich harvests, they will think of how they had to till the fields.

A similar thing happens when we enjoy God's gifts. Quickly we can push Him to the fringes of our mind, and we conclude that human ability has brought us these good things. Our thriving business is the result of careful planning, hard work, and dedication. Our solid relationship with God is a credit to the effort we're putting into it by reading the Scriptures, praying regularly, and going to church. Our well-behaved children are the product of the many parenting books we have read and the seminars we have attended. In short, it's something we have done.

Whenever we are tempted to take the credit, Moses says, "You shall remember the LORD your God, for it is He who gives you power to get wealth, that He may establish His covenant" (Deut. 8:18). God gives the ability for every good human activity: for studying, for parenting, for working, for serving in the community or church. Yes, He wants us to steward our gifts and opportunities in a responsible and faithful way. But when He blesses us, we must humbly recognize that God is being good and gracious: "Gratitude generates humility which...leads believers to concede that they are far from self-sufficient."[17]

Recall the probing question: "What do you have that you did not receive?" And recall the pointed follow-up question: "Now if you did indeed receive it, why do you boast as if you had not received it?" (1 Cor. 4:7). There is no room for boasting, but we should give all the tribute to God. Everything we have is a gift of grace, and we must honestly confess that we deserve nothing.

Discontentment

It is hard to be content. To accept my position in life—what I have, and where I am going—to accept all this from the Father's hand and live at peace, this is contentment. It means that I don't constantly long for more or become jealous of others but that I am satisfied and thankful in the Lord. Yet contentment isn't easy. Flashing in front of our eyes are beautiful and exciting things that are available for purchase. Today we are constantly being updated on what everyone else is doing and buying. We get an online portrait of how interesting and exciting and happy their lives seem—especially compared to our own boring existence. Have you acquired this? Have you been here? Are you sure that you have enough?

---

17. DeJong, *Eucharistic Reciprocity*, 224.

And if we're not content, and we don't feel like we have enough, we're going to suspend our gratitude. When we have a scarcity mindset, habitually finding that our present blessings are inadequate, we won't be inclined to live in gratitude to God. Charles Spurgeon observed, "You say, 'If I had a little more, I should be very satisfied.' You make a mistake. If you are not content with what you have, you would not be satisfied if it were doubled."[18]

Like so many of our problems, this one springs from our sinful heart. By nature, ours is a heart that doesn't rest easy, that wants more: "Dissatisfaction at one's lot, and a disposition to be discontented with things that come to us in the providence of God, are foes to gratitude and enemies to thanksgiving."[19] But God wants us to turn our eyes away from the things that we do not have and to look at what we do have, which are often the truly necessary things. Even if we don't have endless resources, Paul says, "having food and clothing, with these we shall be content" (1 Tim. 6:8).

In Philippians 4, Paul refers to contentment as something he had to work at. He says in verse 12, "Everywhere and in all things I have *learned* both to be full and to be hungry, both to abound and to suffer need." It is striking that he wrote Philippians when he was in a Roman jail. As he sat there, the possibility of death was very much in his thoughts. Yet he wasn't paralyzed with fear. He was grateful for the Philippians' concern and support while he was in prison. Even in his woeful condition, Paul affirms, "I have learned in whatever state I am, to be content" (v. 11). He could be at peace, well-satisfied, "in whatever state."

Was Paul a super-Christian, somehow immune to life's troubles? No. Can we share in this kind of peace? Yes, because we have access to contentment's true source: "I can do all things through Christ who strengthens me" (v. 13). Printed on myriad bookmarks and mugs, this text is justly known and loved by many. But together with Paul's

---

18. Charles Haddon Spurgeon, "The Bed and Its Covering," Sermons, The Spurgeon Center for Biblical Preaching at Midwestern Seminary, https://www.spurgeon.org/resource-library/sermons/the-bed-and-its-covering/#flipbook/.

19. Bounds, "Essentials of Prayer," 307.

personal testimony to his contentment, these words are even more remarkable: Paul was at rest because he knew the abiding strength of the Lord Jesus. There is a strength that is sufficient for whatever earthly situation Christ's followers face.

You and I can live in true tranquility of spirit through the same life-restoring and life-sustaining grace of the triune God: "The consideration of the greatness of the mercies that we have, and the littleness of the things that God has denied us, is a very powerful consideration to work this grace of contentment."[20] Whatever our condition and situation, we can be grateful to the God who knows exactly what we need. "When we are content, we spy mercy in every condition and have our hearts laminated with thanksgiving."[21]

A Heart for Praise

We will continue to struggle against the sinful attitudes and wicked tendencies that undermine our gratitude, so it is good to recall again and again (and again) the abundance of all that we have received from God. Earlier I quoted George Herbert's prayer:

> Thou that hast giv'n so much to me,
> Give one thing more—a gratefull heart.

In this prayer is the confession that we need God's help in becoming a more grateful people. And in the following lines of his prayer comes the acknowledgment that true gratitude must be more than an emotional reaction:

> Not thankfull, when it pleaseth me;
> As if Thy blessings had spare dayes,
> But such a heart, whose pulse may be Thy praise.[22]

---

20. Jeremiah Burroughs, *The Rare Jewel of Christian Contentment* (Edinburgh: Banner of Truth, 1964), 208.

21. Erik J. Raymond, *Chasing Contentment: Trusting God in a Discontented Age* (Wheaton, Ill.: Crossway, 2017), 164.

22. Herbert, "Gratefulnesse," 124–25.

One of the themes in this book has been the importance of having eyes open for God's blessings. Being vigilant is essential in the fight against the things that kill our gratitude, such as idolatry, forgetfulness, and discontentment. By being vigilant, we come to see how each one of God's good gifts provides another opportunity for humble thanksgiving. Each one of His gifts stimulates our heart's pulse for praise.

In his book *Letters to Malcolm*, C. S. Lewis reflects on how God prompts our gratitude through His generosity. God doesn't make us thankful by commanding or threatening us. Instead, God seeks to draw gratitude out of us with His good things. Such pleasures become our tutors in thanksgiving.

And in God's school of thanksgiving, we ought to be moved not just by the notable and spectacular. Lewis writes that he tried "to make every pleasure into a channel of adoration."[23] When we are ready to gratefully welcome God's gifts, then "no pleasure [is] too ordinary or too usual for such reception; from the first taste of the air when I look out of the window...down to one's soft slippers at bed-time."[24] No pleasure is too small to announce the kindness and mercy of God. All around us is fuel for the steadily burning fire of thanksgiving if we will but notice and harvest it for the Lord.

Does God command our thankfulness? Yes, but it is not the onerous diktat of a tyrant; it is the loving command of the Father. God's desire is for His children's highest happiness in Him. So He lavishes us with good things for the sake of His Son, and He delights to see us excel in thankfulness.

---

23. C. S. Lewis, *Letters to Malcolm, Chiefly on Prayer* (London: Fontana, 1964), 91.

24. Lewis, *Letters to Malcolm*, 92.

Reflect . . .

◆ What specific graces have you received from God?

◆ What does it mean that you have received kindness from God in Jesus?

◆ Where in your life are you drawn to trust in created things and not the Creator?

◆ What do you expect from God? And what have you received?

◆ What things have you been taking for granted? How can you begin to take them with gratitude instead?

◆ Are you learning to be content?

◆ Through Christ are you finding strength for doing and enduring all things?

CHAPTER 7

How to Excel in Thankfulness

If you have persevered to this chapter, I hope that you'll have begun to see the vital importance of gratitude. Thankfulness expresses a believer's adoration for the triune God, who has promised and done great things. Even so, gratitude is sometimes minimized in the believer's life. It has been asked, "Where does gratitude rank on your list of Christian virtues?"[1] As a virtue, thankfulness does not seem to generate the same excitement as some other significant Spirit-led activities, like mountain-moving faith, global ministry, or spine-tingling worship. In an age when many people—Christians, too—long to be notable, gratitude seems blandly commonplace. Yet Scripture calls us to grow in gratitude, to pursue our life's work of thanksgiving. This means that we should learn to excel in this important virtue.

Most Valuable Thanker

Alongside its frequent command to give thanks to the Lord, Scripture intimates that our thanksgiving should grow. For instance, 2 Corinthians 4:15 says that as God's grace transforms the Corinthian church, it will "cause thanksgiving to *abound* to the glory of God." Paul envisions a burgeoning thanksgiving centered on God's work in Corinth. Grace begets gratitude and in an ever-increasing measure.

Similarly, in Colossians 2:6–7, the Spirit exhorts us to walk in Christ, "rooted and built up in Him and established in the faith, as

---

1. DeMoss, *Choosing Gratitude*, 22.

you have been taught, *abounding in it with thanksgiving.*" Literally, it says that we should "excel" in thanksgiving. This is an unusual image because those who excel typically deserve some recognition. For instance, people honor those who excel at writing novels or playing baseball or selling real estate. You can make a name by being really good at something. On the other hand, thanksgiving goes hand in hand not with praise, but with humility. There are no prizes for gratitude, like "Most Valuable Thanker" or "Top Appreciator."

But the Holy Spirit says, "Excel in thanksgiving!" It's as if He says, "If you are going to be good at something, be good at this. Shine in gratitude. Stand out with your worship." Because you have received everything and are utterly dependent on God, you should become really good at giving glory to God. If there is anything you should be known for, let it be thanksgiving. If you have received Christ, who abounds in every way, then you should abound with thanksgiving.

Consistent with this is the Spirit's command in the following chapter of Colossians: "And whatever you do in word or deed, do all in the name of the Lord Jesus, giving thanks to God the Father through Him" (3:17). This sweeping command says that everything we do should be shaped by thanksgiving.

Excelling in gratitude requires deliberate effort. As with mastering any activity, whether playing the cello or bricklaying or baking bread, it takes continual attention to keep our gratitude conscious and lively. And so in this chapter I will suggest a handful of ways in which we can increase in thankfulness.

See Your Blessings
A few chapters ago, we started making a tally of God's gifts. As a holy habit to develop, it is vital for excelling in thankfulness. But such stocktaking requires us to have open eyes: "The power of gratitude is the ability to see the good."[2] In short, we need to notice the good things all around us.

2. Joshua Choonmin Kang, *Spirituality of Gratitude: The Unexpected Blessings of Thankfulness* (Downers Grove, Ill.: IVP, 2015), 42.

The Holy Spirit says in Colossians 4:2, "Continue earnestly in prayer, *being vigilant in it with thanksgiving*." Essential to the practice of prayer is vigilance, when we pray with a keen watchfulness and attentiveness. Each day we should strive to notice God's goodness and then thank Him for it. M. Craig Barnes writes, "I doubt that there is such a thing as a measure of spirituality, but if there is, gratitude would be it. Only the grateful are paying attention. They are grateful because they pay attention, and they pay attention because they are so grateful."[3] With eyes open for the gifts, we are better prepared to see the Giver.

Quite some time ago, my wife and I read *The Book of Awesome* by Neil Pasricha.[4] In it, he helps people to see and appreciate the many small things in life. We should take joy in the ordinary but awesome things, like enjoying the smell of rain on a hot sidewalk, hitting several green lights in a row, or waking up and realizing that it's Saturday. In the words of the promotional material, "Pasricha reminds us that the best things in life really are free." We enjoyed his book not only for how it made us smile but also for how it encouraged a grateful awareness of so many aspects of our regular existence.

This awareness should be an essential trait for believers. An attentive child of God will see no limit to His generosity. We will find much to fill a prayer of praise: "The person who has chosen to make gratitude his or her mind-set and lifestyle can view anything— *anything!*—through the eyes of thankfulness."[5] As Nouwen writes, "Every gift I acknowledge reveals another and another until, finally, even the most normal, obvious, and seemingly mundane event or encounter proves to be filled with grace."[6]

And so we should take careful notice of the Father's daily generosity. By taking an interest in the little things, we imitate Christ. He was "thankful for five small loaves and two small fish" because

3. M. Craig Barnes, *The Pastor as Minor Poet: Texts and Subtexts in the Ministerial Life* (Grand Rapids: Eerdmans, 2008), 64.
4. Neil Pasricha, *The Book of Awesome* (New York: Berkley Books, 2011).
5. DeMoss, *Choosing Gratitude*, 62, emphasis in original.
6. Nouwen, *Return of the Prodigal Son*, 86.

in this paltry meal He "saw God's abundance."[7] In this connection, the gratitude journals for sale in your local bookstore might help you become more grateful to the God of all grace. For what specific gifts and blessings are you thankful to God? Keep thinking about it until that inventory swells—until it humbles you! And then pray in thanksgiving for God's kindness and unending goodness.

Compiling a list of gifts is no guarantee of increased thanksgiving. Perhaps you've experienced the frustration of contemplating the many things for which you should be grateful, yet you are not feeling thankful. Even so, making a list can be valuable in training us to see God's gifts. I have talked to believers who were sick and dying, yet modeled a grateful spirit. They were insistent on counting their blessings, even the "small things" like a warm house and a good night's sleep and the opportunity to go to church. Above all, their words gave testimony to how they learned to focus not on what is physical or material. They learned to set the eyes of their heart not on the fleeting things that are seen, but on the unseen things that last forever. May we all be vigilant in thanksgiving.

Savor Your Blessings

We tend to take God's gifts for granted. One way to counter this is by pausing to savor His blessings. Linger over them. Enjoy them. Take delight in them. Make time to appreciate God's goodness as you experience it every day of your life. Savoring something means that when one of God's gifts brings us pleasure, we should acknowledge it to the Lord. James writes, "Is anyone cheerful? Let him sing psalms" (James 5:13).

An obvious occasion for savoring God's blessings is in His gift of daily bread. If your household is like ours, then mealtime sometimes feels like a mad rush to inhale the food, with little time for measured chewing. No one likes soggy breakfast cereal or lukewarm mashed potatoes, so we eat in a hurry. But surely our mealtimes could profit from a slower pace to help us enjoy the pleasure of good food. Sit

---

7. Kang, *Spirituality of Gratitude*, 50.

down, slow down, and notice the pleasure of God's gift of food. He has created an amazing variety of tastes and flavors. As the preacher of Ecclesiastes counsels us, "Go, eat your bread with joy, and drink your wine with a merry heart" (9:7). Savor these things as tokens of God's goodness and let them move you to gratitude to God. And here, too, we hear Chestertonian wisdom: "We should thank God for beer and Burgundy by not drinking too much of them."[8] Enjoy in moderation, and then thank God profusely!

Savoring God's blessings—of whatever kind—requires time and attentiveness. When we rush through our days enslaved by the tyranny of the urgent, we probably won't have occasion to enjoy His goodness. But when we reserve time at the margins, we will have space to appreciate the earthy aroma of freshly ground coffee beans, the pure simplicity of a piano sonata, the lively laughter after a good joke, and the stillness of a Sunday evening after a day of worshiping with God's people. Revel in the moment and offer up thanksgiving to God, who is the overflowing fountain of all good: "Oh, taste and see that the LORD is good" (Ps. 34:8).

Pay Attention to Answered Prayers

The children of God are grateful for the privilege of approaching our Father in heaven. God listens, and God answers. As James says, "The effective, fervent prayer of a righteous man avails much" (James 5:16). So another way to cultivate a spirit of gratitude is to take notice of God's answers to our prayers.

We often forget what we asked God for. And even when we receive it, we forget to thank God. We pray for something in the morning, but by the evening, we have already taken it for granted. For instance, we start our day with a prayer for something we call "traveling mercies." The kids are going out the door to school, or Dad is driving to work, or you need to drive for a couple of hours somewhere in the car, and you ask for protection and safety on the roads. And you go out, and you all make it safely home—even after

---

8. G. K. Chesterton, *Orthodoxy* (Chicago: Moody, 2009), 99.

many miles traveled—but there might be little thought to how God actually answered your prayer.

Or we ask God for strength in doing what we need to do. We pray that He would keep us from willful sin, or give the endurance to stand at the front of the classroom all day, or grant wisdom for a three-hour meeting, or supply courage to face that appointment with the specialist. Then we journey through our day without committing a grievous sin or melting into a puddle of fear or anxiety. Actually, we enjoy our work, we get good news from the doctor, and we have the chance to bless someone with our words. God provided everything that we asked for and needed and much more. But do we take the time to thank Him? Or did we assume that we would get it anyway?

We show gratitude to God by seeing when He answers us. Remember what you prayed for, and then remember to thank God for His blessings. Isaac Watts says about gratitude in prayer: "In our thanksgiving, we should be sure to take notice of all responses to prayer, all merciful appearances of God in answer to our requests. For it is but a poor converse maintained with God if we care only about our speaking to him, but take no notice of any replies he condescends to make to our poor and worthless addresses."[9] Celebrate how God has graciously answered your prayers.

And even when we haven't asked for His gifts, God bestows blessing. "Perhaps we never specifically asked God for these blessings or for thousands of others today, but God graciously gave them to us anyway."[10] Especially God's gift of reconciliation and salvation was not something for which we asked. Indeed, we would never have conceived of such an amazing restoration of our lost condition. But God has been immensely gracious in Christ Jesus, so we thank Him.

As we become more aware of God's relentless generosity and His often unsought favor, we give Him praise. "Wherever there is true

---

9. Watts, *Guide to Prayer*, 118.
10. Beeke and Beeke, *Developing a Healthy Prayer Life*, 33.

prayer, there thanksgiving and gratitude stand by, ready to respond to the answer when it comes."[11]

Notice Your Neighbor

As a pastor, I have been invited to attend many wedding receptions. One of the touching moments is when a best man or maid of honor, a parent or sibling, takes the microphone to speak some words of appreciation about the bride or groom. They might share some cherished memories, reflect on the person's endearing qualities, or speak with gratitude for their godly friendship. The love and gratitude are palpable.

Listening to the heartfelt words, I sometimes wonder if we do this kind of thing enough. It shouldn't take an available microphone, a glass of wine, and a sentimental evening for us to be thankful for other people—and to tell them that we are thankful. When I asked folks about their reasons for gratitude, this was certainly a common theme: they were grateful for dear friends, for godly parents, for devoted siblings, for a loving husband or wife.

God wants us to find comfort and encouragement through the gift of other people. Scripture gives many examples of gratefully recognizing this gift. Paul regularly begins his letters with thanksgiving for God's work. And it is striking that his thanksgiving is not generic but crafted to match the particular way in which God is working among the believers. For instance, Paul expresses gratitude for the Ephesians: "Therefore I also, after I heard of your faith in the Lord Jesus and your love for all the saints, do not cease to give thanks for you, making mention of you in my prayers" (Eph. 1:15–16).[12] In their conversion the apostle sees a beautiful display of God's powerful work. For this grace he has not stopped thanking the Lord.

This kind of gratitude redirects our attention toward others. Thank God for what He is busy doing in the people in your life. It

---

11. Bounds, "Essentials of Prayer," 308.
12. There are other examples of apostolic appreciation for people, such as Romans 1:8 and 2 Thessalonians 1:3–4 (see also 1 Cor. 1:4; Phil. 1:3; Col. 1:3).

shouldn't require special occasions—weddings, birthdays, anniversaries, Father's and Mother's Days, or even funerals—to realize how God is working in other people and perhaps blessing us through them. As I said in a previous chapter, we shouldn't take our loved ones for granted but treasure them as God's gifts.

And then remember again that our thankfulness should extend past those people with whom we share living quarters, DNA, or loyalty to a sports team. Think of your family in Christ, those fellow believers in your congregation or those you know from other contexts. Don Carson puts to us:

> For what have we thanked God recently? Have we gone over a list of members at our local church, say, or over a list of Christian workers, and quietly thanked God for signs of grace in their lives? Do we make it a matter of praise to God when we observe evidence in one another of growing conformity to Christ, exemplified in trust, reliability, love, and genuine spiritual stamina?[13]

Thank the Lord for all the good and faithful work that He is doing in the church of which you are part, locally and around the world.

Reframe What Is Difficult

God brings troubles into the lives of each of His children. Such difficulties are a real challenge to our spirit of gratitude. In the next chapter, we'll consider how we can give thanks in all circumstances, even those rife with tears and heartache. Jesus promised that we will have trouble in this world (John 16:33), yet for those who know Him, no trouble is so troublesome that it means God has withdrawn His love. And so we reframe our circumstances in light of the Father's ongoing care.

Reframing means that we try to view our struggles with a better and sanctified understanding. We know that this hardship is God's perfect counsel for us (Ps. 33:11). We also trust that nothing can separate us from God's love (Rom. 8:38–39). What is more, we are

---

13. Carson, *Praying with Paul*, 26.

sure that God is using this difficulty to teach us (Heb. 12:7–11), and we remember that God has promised to always provide, day by day (Matt. 6:31–33). We strive to look at our circumstances with this new and heavenly perspective.

I encountered this kind of reframing when I read the novel *Robinson Crusoe* by Daniel Defoe. This tale of a sailor marooned on an island is well known. Perhaps less well known is how Crusoe grew in his Christian faith during his trials. An important strategy for him was to reframe his miseries to grow in gratitude. In Crusoe's words,

> As my reason began now to master my despondency, I began to comfort myself as well as I could, and to set the good against the evil, that I might have something to distinguish my case from worse; and I stated it very impartially, like debtor and creditor, the comforts I enjoyed, against the miseries I suffered, thus:

EVIL	GOOD
I am cast upon a horrible desolate island, void of all hope of recovery.	But I am alive, and not drowned, as all ship's company was.
I am singled out and separated, as it were, from all the world to be miserable.	But I am singled out too from all the ship's crew to be spared from death; and He that miraculously saved me from death can deliver me from this condition.
I have no clothes to cover me.	But I am in a hot climate, where if I had clothes, I could hardly wear them.
I am without any defense or means to resist any violence of man or beast.	But I am cast on an island, where I see no wild beasts to hurt me, as I saw on the coast of Africa. And what if I had been shipwrecked there?[14]

14. Daniel Defoe, *Robinson Crusoe* (Mahwah, N.J.: Watermill, 1980), 96–97.

Remarkably, Crusoe was determined to remain grateful by regarding his plight in a more positive light. Our favorite gratitude commentator, G. K. Chesterton, picked up on Crusoe's reframing too: "Even the pessimist when he thinks, if he ever does, must realise that he has something to be thankful for: he owes something to the world, as Robinson Crusoe did to the ship. You may regard the universe as a wreck: but at least you have saved something from the wreck."[15]

When we yearn to excel in gratitude, we'll try to reframe our difficult circumstances so that they resemble opportunities. Understand it well: this reframing does not depend on our ability to think laterally or on our resilience or our cheery disposition. We can reframe our situation because we know the power and goodness of God. His mercies are new every morning, even on those mornings that dawn dark and gray in our hearts. This truth sanctifies our perspective and instills a persistent gratitude. Even in difficult times, we know God is busy with us and is bringing to completion the good work that He has started.

Speak of Your Blessings
We speak about what we cherish. A football fanatic will love to recount the greatest games won by his team. A bibliophile will speak of the latest books acquired and read. A lovestruck suitor will find any occasion to mention his stunning belle and her finest qualities. Jesus put it best: "For out of the abundance of the heart his mouth speaks" (Luke 6:45).

In learning to excel in gratitude, we acknowledge aloud how God has blessed us. For instance, the psalmist announces, "Come and hear, all you who fear God, *and I will declare what He has done for my soul*" (Ps. 66:16). He wants to speak about how the Lord has answered his prayers with great works of deliverance. The psalmist gives God the glory for all that He has accomplished.

Some people love to tell about their thanks. Maybe you know someone who needs no prompt at all to speak about the blessings

15. Chesterton, "The Idea of Separation and the Sense of Separateness," in *Collected Works*, 28:202.

of the Lord. Gratitude just arises naturally from his or her lips in the middle of conversation:

> "It's a blessing how God has encouraged me lately through the Psalms."

> "I am so grateful for the support of my children."

> "Isn't all this rain we've been having such a gift from the Lord?"

Others of us are more hesitant to verbalize our gratitude to God—not that we don't see His gifts or savor them. Perhaps we just don't feel comfortable to speak about them.

But it is good to speak of our blessings. The experts tell us that the act of speaking about things is a powerful way to shape our thinking. To talk about something gratefully requires us to pause, to meditate (even for a moment), and to articulate what it is that we value about this person or that experience or some gift. Speaking positively and thankfully trains our mind to travel the paths of gratitude. Speaking shapes our seeing.

This acknowledgment helps us. It helps the people around us, setting an example for our children and encouraging our fellow believers. More importantly, speaking about our blessings brings praise to God. In a sense, almost every psalm is a celebration of the Lord's gifts, but Psalm 107 is a particularly good example. From beginning to end, the psalmist thankfully recounts God's great works of salvation. And he exhorts everyone to respond rightly to the Lord: "Let them sacrifice the sacrifices of thanksgiving, *and declare His works with rejoicing*" (v. 22). If you're thankful, tell someone. If your heart is full of God's goodness, let it come out. By declaring God's works, we learn to excel in gratitude.

Remember God's Past Gifts

Spiritual amnesia is our tendency to forget the fundamental truths of God's Word. We forget about who God is, who we are, and what He has done for us in Christ. And when we forget, we are often in real danger of falling into the sin of ingratitude.

So another way to excel in thanksgiving is to develop our memories for God's great gifts. Memory nourishes gratitude, serves as a great aid to our faith, and prompts our praise. You might have thanked God in the moment of receiving or enjoying. But do it again when you reflect on His answer to prayer in the coming days, weeks, and years. As often as you remember how God helped and provided, thank Him.

For God's people, this is a sure pathway to hope. We sometimes lurch from one worry to the next. We find a new reason for anxiety almost as soon as the previous one disappears. In our natural fear and fretfulness, there can be moments and days when all seems lost and futile. But then we recall "the years of the right hand of the Most High" (Ps. 77:10). And we are confident that this misery, too, will pass. I am sure that this darkness will lift because of God and His great faithfulness.

Remembering God's past mercies is not just an activity for senior believers. Older Christians can certainly give a testimony to long decades of God's care. They witness to the fact that no matter what happened, the Lord was steadfast. Even when dementia has set in, these brothers and sisters cling to the simple truths of the gospel. We ought to listen to them and be encouraged. But any child of God can recall what God has done. We remember His works throughout the years of our life—how God guided, blessed, answered, strengthened, disciplined, provided, and comforted. Positive memories of the Lord's goodness are like a reservoir on which we can draw for future praise.

Even when difficult things trouble our memory, we see how God's abiding hand was present. We are thankful for how, in our difficulty, God sustained us faithfully. Looking back, we are grateful for those times of apparent hopelessness when the Lord delivered us yet again. Also, when we recall with shame the ugly sins of our past, we remember how God showed mercy (see Ps. 25:7). A beautiful Puritan prayer expresses such gratitude: "The memory of my great sins, my many temptations, my falls, bring afresh into my mind the remembrance of thy great help, of thy support from heaven, of the great grace that saved such a wretch as I am."[16] We remember, and we give thanks.

What If You Had Not Received...?

Much earlier in this book, we reflected on the question, "What do you have that you did not receive?" (1 Cor. 4:7). The activity of seeing and savoring God's blessings is a sure prompt to gratitude. But a variation on the question might also be helpful: What if you had *not* received...? Choose one or more of God's blessings to you, and then try to imagine what life would be like if God had not given them. For instance,

> What if I had not received two working legs?
> What if the Lord had not been on our side?
> What if I did not belong to a loving church community?
> What if I didn't have the Bible as a light to my path?
> What if I did not have gainful employment?
> What if I knew about God, but did not have faith?
> What if I had not married my spouse?
> What if I did not reside in a country ruled by law
> and order?

For most readers these are probably hypothetical questions, so they may struggle to answer. And sometimes God does withhold blessings, such as health, or a spouse, or children, or peace. In the next chapter, we'll consider whether we can still be grateful when God does not grant our heart's desire, particularly when it is a good and God-honoring desire. But when we have long enjoyed God's varied gifts, we can't imagine life without them. Yet when we try to ponder their absence, we start to realize how precious they really are. Without these blessings—mundane as they sometimes appear—we would struggle in unspeakable ways. So we should thank God for what He has given.

---

16. Bennett, *Valley of Vision*, 71.

The frightening (though mercifully unlikely) prospect of losing God's blessings reminds us of how Asaph meditates on his trouble in Psalm 77:7–9. Mired in a dark place, he poses six loaded questions:

> Will the Lord cast off forever?
> And will He be favorable no more?
> Has His mercy ceased forever?
> Has His promise failed forevermore?
> Has God forgotten to be gracious?
> Has He in anger shut up His tender mercies?

A yes to any of these queries would mean that all hope is lost. But listening to Asaph's questions, we hear the answers whispered between the lines. "Will the Lord cast off forever?" (v. 7). No, for He is faithful. "And will He be favorable no more?" (v. 7). No, for God is full of grace. "Has His mercy ceased forever?" (v. 8). No, His mercies are new every morning. We could lose our legs, our job, or our freedom, but we cannot lose our salvation. The Lord will not cast us off. And so we are grateful.

If we had not received God's grace in Christ, we would be nothing. And God knows that we can't bring anything to repay His abounding goodness. Yet we are left with one principal task. It's why we are here: to abound with thanksgiving to our triune God. So get really good at it. Shine in your praise and excel in gratitude.

Reflect ...

♦ Are you good at gratitude? Why or why not?

♦ What steps can you take to begin excelling in thanksgiving?

♦ Where can you improve in the practice of thanking God?

♦ What if you woke up today and all you had were the things you thanked God for yesterday?

In All Circumstances

I begin this penultimate chapter with a *but*: But can a person *always* be thankful? We've spent a lot of time in this book counting and celebrating the good things of the Lord. We have marveled at how God blesses us with myriad gifts. Everywhere we turn, there are blessings to see, to savor, to speak about, and to share.

But life isn't always so cheery and bright. We are accustomed to eliminating most inconveniences and discomforts from our day through using the latest gadgets and taking the right pharmaceuticals. Our preference is for a pain-free existence. Scripture's teaching, however, is that suffering is assured. Jesus tells His followers, "In the world you will have tribulation" (John 16:33). And it is the hard truth that we hear in Job: "Man is born to trouble, as the sparks fly upward" (Job 5:7).

And suffering does come: trouble in our mental and physical health, strife in our relationships, stress on finances, division in the local church, and all the temptations and hostility of living in an unbelieving world. In such times, we still know that God is good, but His goodness can seem unreal or inaccessible. A person might make a long inventory of God's gifts, even keep a daily diary of blessings, yet feel utterly miserable. Perhaps she even feels worse for having received so much yet still being bereft of gratitude.

For Christians who are in the turmoil of hardship, God's grace can appear as a distant reality. Believers might be frustrated with God, disappointed with Him, even angry—they don't *want* to be thankful. Being grateful can seem like an impossibility when our outlook is clouded by chronic pain or anxiety for tomorrow or fear or regret. Any talk of gratitude seems facile—or worse, cruel. So can a person thank the Lord always?

When Gratitude Is Hard

For this book the Lord's command in 1 Thessalonians 5:18 has been foundational: "Give thanks." It is a message that is easy to echo, to print on mugs and cell phone wallpapers. But two additional words in that verse transform it into a serious challenge: *in everything*. This makes an ordinary command—something that even nonbelievers agree is healthy and polite—far more difficult. God calls us to give thanks not only at the end of a productive day at work nor only for a savory meatloaf or an encouraging sermon. He says, "In everything give thanks."

This has always been a tough assignment for believers. For the Thessalonians who were first addressed by the apostle's command, it meant they had to give thanks even as they endured the trial of persecution (1 Thess. 2:14–15). The Thessalonians had to give thanks, even when they attended the funeral of yet another brother or sister in Christ (4:13).

For us, too, this command means being grateful even when we don't feel grateful. James exhorts, "Count it all joy when you fall into various trials" (James 1:2). But can you really count it all joy during a long season of pain and suffering? Or can you be grateful when your life seems like it's collapsing in a heap? How can we give thanks when we don't know how we're going to pay this tax bill, meet this work deadline, or deal with this family brokenness? Gratitude is sorely challenged by the presence of hardship.

What makes gratitude so hard during our trials? Perhaps we think that we deserve a better lot than we have been getting. Or perhaps we compare ourselves with others nearby who are enjoying many good things. Or we feel that God hasn't been honest with us, that He hasn't delivered on the blessings He promised. We prayed in our day of trouble but received no answer. We looked for His good purpose in all this, but it still seems pointless and empty. And the simple fact is, receiving good things is enjoyable, and savoring food and friends and freedom is pleasant. Meanwhile, we struggle to see what can possibly be good about our current trouble. We cannot pretend that thanksgiving in all circumstances is going to be straightforward. Nouwen writes about how gratitude involves making a conscious choice to see and to trust in the goodness of the Lord, to turn to Him even during the dark night of tribulation. This will be difficult, but the alternative is even worse: "I can choose to dwell in the darkness in which I stand, point to those who are seemingly better off than I, lament about the many misfortunes that have plagued me in the past, and thereby wrap myself up in my resentment."[1] Such an approach will never lead to joy in the Lord. Instead, it is God's will for us to live in the peace of a grateful spirit.

Appreciation Recalibrations

So how can we nurture gratitude in everything, even in adversity? Perhaps we try to make a mental adjustment or two, recalibrating ourselves toward thankfulness. The first adjustment is to evaluate our hardship in comparison to our other blessings. To put it another way, I can remain thankful if I feel that the good things in my life still outweigh the bad. Flannery O'Connor, an American author, wrote this as her health was steadily deteriorating: "I have enough energy to write with and as that is all I have any business doing anyhow, I can with one eye squinted take it all as a blessing."[2] Despite her trouble, she recognized that there was still a greater good.

This determination to be grateful is commendable. We should strive to remain aware of God's gifts in every circumstance. But there may be dark times in life when the bad and the difficult really do seem to outweigh anything that is good. We should not trust God because

---

1. Nouwen, *Return of the Prodigal Son*, 85.
2. Flannery O'Connor, *The Habit of Being: Letters of Flannery O'Connor* (New York: Farrar, Straus and Giroux, 1988), xvi.

we always find that on balance "it works out." We will need a surer basis for thankfulness in suffering, which we will come to shortly.

When we're under duress, there is a second recalibration toward gratitude. This involves thinking of someone who is worse off than we are. A few pages ago, we saw how the shipwrecked Robinson Crusoe reframed his troubles. As he put it, "I learned here again to observe that it is very rare that the providence of God casts us into any condition of life so low, or any misery so great, but we may see something or other to be thankful for; *and may see others in worse circumstances than our own.*"[3] Parents have been known to give counsel in a spirit similar to Crusoe to their complaining children: "Kids, just think of the poor children in Africa. They don't get to eat fresh vegetables every day like you do. So eat up!" This is true—in the world there are many who lack basic amenities. There can be benefit in reflecting on how little so many other people have compared to us.

But what if we're not acquainted with any notable sufferers? What if the African orphan remains only a vague reality to our minds? This pathway to gratitude seems ambiguous or unreliable. As explained in the previous chapter, it is better to reframe our situation through confessing God's power and abiding goodness. This truth sanctifies our perspective. Even in difficult times, we know that God is busy with us and is bringing to completion the good work that He has started. The God of all grace makes it possible to be truly thankful in all circumstances. Nowhere is this clearer than in the story of Job.

Job's Gratitude

The story of Job is old, possibly one of the oldest in the Scriptures. His tale is introduced in the first two chapters of the book bearing his name. The trouble starts when Satan's attention is directed to this righteous and prosperous man. With the Lord's permission, Satan brutally assaults Job. He wants to see if Job's faith will endure even when God's hedge of protection is removed and life gets a lot harder.

---

3. DeFoe, *Robinson Crusoe*, 274; emphasis added.

So in due course, Job loses all his material wealth and earthly possessions. Not a few hours later, all of Job's children are killed in a terrible disaster. At the end of that dark day, Job nevertheless praises God and acknowledges His sovereign power. Job had received much, he had lost much, but he will glorify God's name: "The LORD gave, and the LORD has taken away; blessed be the name of the LORD" (Job 1:21).

Satan is not done yet, however. He is also allowed to take away Job's physical health. Job is left a miserable shadow of his former self, afflicted with sores from head to toe. This is too much for Job's wife, who urges him to curse God and meet his end. Yet Job keeps the faith. He affirms the rightness of humbly submitting to the Lord's perfect will: "Shall we indeed accept good from God, and shall we not accept adversity?" (Job 2:10).

Job is a remarkable example of tenacious gratitude and resolute contentment. These words describe him well: "Even while encountering a season of intense difficulty, the contented person may still—because contentment is a work of grace from the inside out—have his or her heart dilated in thankfulness."[4] At his lowest, Job will continue to bless the God of all grace.

But Job's anguish has only just begun. In the aftermath of his trauma, the trouble really comes. Particularly when his friends attempt to comfort him, painful questions arise about God's justice and goodness.

After several rounds of dialogue that at times are harsh and even merciless, Job feels utterly alone in his hour of need. In chapter 19 he says he is cut off from his brothers, his acquaintances, his relatives, his hired servants—even his wife and close friends (vv. 13–19). But he also makes a startling confession. Job has one friend, a helper on high: "I know that my Redeemer lives, and He shall stand at last on the earth" (v. 25). Somehow, even in his darkest hour, Job knows that he isn't alone. Forsaken by every earthly companion, chastised by the

---

4. Raymond, *Chasing Contentment*, 165.

Lord in heaven, he still has a Redeemer. He can still look to the One
who will take up his cause and plead for him to God.

It is one of this ancient book's great mysteries. Who was Job's
Redeemer? We immediately think of Jesus the Mediator, the one in
God's presence who lives to make intercession. But Job didn't know
the name of Christ. He surely remembered that God had promised
a Savior centuries before (Gen. 3:15), yet he didn't understand what
this meant. Job peered ahead and saw only a shadowy silhouette of
the One who was coming. And this was enough. In his trouble, Job
knew that help was on the way. Even if he died, he had a Redeemer
who would live on and intercede with God in Job's behalf.

After his beautiful confession in chapter 19, Job still has a difficult road to travel. There will be more accusations from his friends.
There will be an admonition from God when the Lord rattles Job
with a powerful revelation of His sovereign glory. And by the end of
the book, there still won't be an answer for every hard question. But
God will have revealed His glorious character and loving heart. The
story concludes with God restoring Job to health and granting new
wealth and more children. As James writes so aptly, "You have heard
of the perseverance of Job and seen the end intended by the Lord—
that the Lord is very compassionate and merciful" (James 5:11).

The book of Job is full of insight and encouragement for any
believer. But especially for those who suffer, Job offers a profoundly
reassuring message. It is honest about the anguish that children of
God sometimes endure. It asks the kinds of difficult questions that
sufferers ask about divine justice, human responsibility, and the purpose of pain. And it also shows that many of these questions cannot
be answered in this life. Even so, Job's steadfast thankfulness to God
the gracious Giver shines bright. It is a powerful example for all who
weep and writhe, a model of how "gratitude can survive the pain of
loss, though it is muted, sung in a lower key."[5]

Job's story doesn't guarantee that there will be earthly restoration after loss. God doesn't always heal. Sometimes God grants no

---

5. DeJong, *Eucharistic Reciprocity*, 232.

child, even though a husband and wife plead for years. Family tension might not subside, though we're sure we could serve God better if He gave us peace. Even so, Job shows that in the pain, we can focus on the sovereignty and goodness of God as our one hope: "The LORD gave, and the LORD has taken away; blessed be the name of the LORD" (Job 1:21). And besides everything else, Job reveals the sure promise of a Redeemer who restores us in the way that matters most.

Lamenting and Looking to Christ

God gives a daunting assignment in 1 Thessalonians 5:18: "In everything give thanks." At times in life, this task can seem impossible and the command heartless. But the key that unlocks this verse comes in its next phrase: "for this is the will of God *in Christ Jesus* for you." In short, it is through our union with Christ that we may always live in gratitude to God.

For the sake of His Son, God has been good to us beyond anything we could have dared to imagine or request. In Christ, God is the Father who loves us. He keeps His promises, and He gives good gifts to His children. Because we know this God, we trust in Him. And so "the giving of thanks in a disappointing or difficult situation is always to be done by faith in the promises of God."[6] We are thankful because, in Christ, God meets our deepest need for deliverance from death, for unchanging truth, and eternal salvation.

Christ Himself could rejoice in His sufferings. Even during all His earthly trouble, the possibility of saving sinners gave Christ great delight: "For the joy that was set before Him [He] endured the cross, despising the shame" (Heb. 12:2). Salvation was the goal, the endgame, the beautiful culmination of His labor of love, and so He rejoiced.

Through His past suffering, Christ is now able to sympathize with those in agony and distress (Heb. 4:15). "Let the one who suffers pain say these things to himself: 'O my Saviour, you understand my sufferings. I thank you that in your exaltation you feel for me. I

---

6. Bridges, *Respectable Sins*, 86.

comfort myself in the sweet condescension and sympathy of your love.'"[7] In our pain, Christ stands with us. He gives us a hope that is steadfast, eternal, and worthy of our thanksgiving.

This transformation of grief into gratitude is written deeply into all the Scriptures. It is well known that many of the psalms—some scholars estimate no fewer than fifty—can be considered laments. This illustrates the truth and reality of suffering for the Lord's people. Yet the biblical laments almost never end without hope. A promise of thanksgiving concludes many of the individual laments in the Psalms.[8] Even before the crisis is resolved, the psalmist offers thanksgiving to God in anticipation. For instance, when David complains to the Lord about the attacks of his enemies in Psalm 35, he is confident of God's good answer. So as he laments, he also resolves to thank Him publicly: "I will give You thanks in the great assembly; I will praise You among many people" (v. 18).

For the Christian reader of the Psalms, the sure shift from lament to gratitude is greatly encouraging. We are mindful that all the psalms—also the many laments—are fulfilled in Christ and point to His gospel (Luke 24:44). Through His saving work, He has already redeemed us, body and soul, from all His and our enemies. In keeping with His promise, Christ is bringing us to completion. Even as we lament, we give thanks, for this is the good will of God in Christ Jesus for us.

Trusting God's Providence

What was the firm foundation underpinning not only Job's gratitude but also the lamenting psalmist's confidence and Christ's joy when enduring His cross? It was a sure trust in God's providence, for He works all things according to the counsel of His will (Eph. 1:11). We know that nothing falls outside His care as Almighty God and faithful Father. Providence means that God is not only in control of our

---

7. P. B. Power, *A Book of Comfort for Those in Sickness* (Edinburgh: Banner of Truth, 2018), 31.

8. See Peter Craigie, *Psalms 1–50*, Word Biblical Commentary 19 (Waco, Tex.: Word Books, 1983), 237–40.

circumstance, but He is in control for our benefit. He is good, and He does what is good (Ps. 119:68).

Affirming God's providence transforms our view of times of prosperity and adversity. His hand directs every event. Particularly regarding hardship, we can ask the question of 1 Corinthians 4:7: "What do you have that you did not receive?" And then we can acknowledge that even our trouble has come to us from the heavenly Father. Dietrich Bonhoeffer gave beautiful expression to this truth in his poem "Powers of Good." He wrote these words in prison at the beginning of 1945, the year in which he would be killed for his part in a plot to assassinate Hitler:

> Should it be ours to drain the cup of grieving
> even to the dregs of pain, at thy command,
> we will not falter, thankfully receiving
> all that is given by thy loving hand.[9]

God knows perfectly what we need when we need it, and He is fully able to bring it about. Resolutely looking to Him, we can be patient in adversity. Says Tim Keller, "Because God is sovereign we are to thank him—we are to live thankfully because we know he is like this. We are to thank him beforehand, even as we make our requests. We are to thank him for whatever he sends to us, even if we don't understand it."[10] When we view our life as firmly in the grip of God's wise providence, we can be content to receive everything from Him in a spirit of thanksgiving.

The School of Suffering

Our trust in God's providence is bolstered by knowing that He is pleased to use all our circumstances to teach, shape, and refine us. This is the meaning of the startling saying in Romans 5:3: "We also glory in tribulations." The Greek word for *tribulation* means

---

9. Bonhoeffer, *Letters and Papers from Prison*, 400.
10. Tim Keller, *Walking with God through Pain and Suffering* (London: Hodder & Stoughton, 2013), 302.

something akin to manual pressure, like squeezing a fresh orange until the juice starts flowing. Sickness and bereavement and anxiety can certainly feel like pressure, a constricting of our life, a heaviness that doesn't go away.

But we can glory in tribulation because God has said it has great value. Having justified us by faith in Christ (Rom. 5:1), God now wants to shape us in conformity to Christ. We are allowed to enter the school of sanctified suffering. Here awaits an entire curriculum to be learned.

Paul says our training begins like this: "Tribulation produces perseverance" (Rom. 5:3). Going through a trial can slowly extend our ability to be patient, and it can fortify our commitment to the Lord. Compare it to weight training: if you apply resistance to a muscle, it can be uncomfortable and even painful, but the result is a stronger muscle. When we are in financial trouble, have anxiety about our children, or are enduring another spell of migraines, God gives an opportunity to depend on Him even more.

Along the way, you might say that God is "squeezing us empty." He is emptying us of things like our pride, our trust in other people, and our security in material things. God may keep applying the pressure until we learn that in ourselves, we have nothing—until we realize that we *are* nothing. As we go through affliction and distress, by His grace we become more reliant on Him, our Father in Christ. In Him we persevere!

Such "perseverance [produces] character" (Rom. 5:4). *Character* is the good quality of something that has been put to the test, like metals that have been put through intense fire. The imperfections are burned off, the elements are refined, and there is a new glow through refining. Peter writes about the believer's purification through trials: "In all this you greatly rejoice, though now for a little while you may have had to suffer grief in all kinds of trials. These have come so that the proven genuineness of your faith—of greater worth than gold, which perishes even though refined by fire—may result in praise, glory and honor when Jesus Christ is revealed" (1 Peter 1:6–7 NIV).

Having been proved genuine in hardship, we thank God for sustaining grace.

And when our character has been tested in trial, by God's grace it produces "hope" (Rom. 5:4). Biblical hope is the confident expectation of what God has promised. Tribulation shifts our gaze away from this present earth and toward eternity. While life can be full of the blessings of good gifts and wonderful people, hardship teaches that the present life is only temporary. As Jeremiah Burroughs put it in his marvelous book on contentment: "The other things are pretty fine indeed, and I should be glad if God would give me them, a fine house, and income, and clothes, and advancement for my wife and children: these are comfortable things, but they are not the necessary things; I may have these and yet perish forever, but the other is absolutely necessary."[11]

The "other" thing that is "absolutely necessary" is our eternal salvation through faith in Christ. God teaches us that this is our better and more enduring hope. As 2 Corinthians 4:18 says, "We do not look at the things which are seen, but at the things which are not seen. For the things which are seen are temporary, but the things which are not seen are eternal." For this unseen reality we hope.

Remembering how God exhorts us to give thanks *in everything*, C. S. Lewis comments, "We ought to give thanks for all fortune: if it is good, because it is good, if bad, because it works in us patience, humility and the contempt of this world and the hope of our eternal country."[12] When we have finished our training in the school of suffering, we will finally graduate to glory.

Staying Thankful amid Suffering

I realize that in my life I have not yet suffered much. And so I posed this question to my brothers and sisters in Christ who have faced various hardships. Some of these trials were (or still are) unimaginably

---

11. Burroughs, *Rare Jewel*, 92–93.
12. C. S. Lewis to Don Giovanni Calabria, August 10, 1948, in *The Quotable Lewis*, ed. Wayne Martindale and Jerry Root (Carol Stream, Ill.: Tyndale, 1990), 579.

difficult. When battling stage 4 cancer, dealing with the long-term
effects of a traumatic car accident, living with the burden of chronic
pain, or facing a bitter disappointment in their family, could they
still be thankful to God? What were they thankful for? By His grace,
these sanctified sufferers were grateful for much.

More than a few thanked God for the support of their family and
the communion of saints. They gratefully recalled hospital rooms
that were crowded with well-wishers and fridges that were full of
home-cooked meals.

One brother was thankful for the grace to patiently accept God's
will, though God had willed for him to spend most of his adult life
in a wheelchair.

Another spoke gratefully of how his suffering with depression
made him more understanding toward those who live with similar
burdens and how it equipped him to minister God's comfort to them.

A sister thanked the Lord for the gift of a good night's sleep, even
when her days were filled with stress and anxiety.

Another rejoiced in how her love for God had deepened during
many months of uncertainty, and how her knowledge of His attributes was marvelously broadened.

Another was helped in her frailty by meditating on the reality of
God's protecting angels.

Many thanked God for the blessing of expert and effective medical care.

One brother spoke of his gratitude for still being able to go to
church every Sunday and listen to the preaching of the gospel.

A sister facing terminal cancer thanked God for the opportunity
to impress on her children that only one thing really matters in life:
knowing and loving God.

These sufferers thanked God for the small and ordinary but precious routines of each day: going for a short walk every morning,
reading the Bible at mealtimes, and welcoming the children home
from school.

Even with tears in their eyes, my brothers and sisters gave thanks for how their suffering had inspired a real hope for the coming kingdom of Christ.

Theirs is surely the kind of thankfulness of which C. S. Lewis spoke: "We shall not be able to adore God on the highest occasions if we have learned no habit of doing so on the lowest."[13] For even when at their lowest, humanly speaking, these saints resolutely gave thanks to God. It is a gratitude we would all do well to emulate. We would not choose suffering, but through it we often experience the Lord's grace more fully.

A suffering child of God may learn to affirm the deepest reason for gratitude. Even in grief and pain, we realize that we can be thankful for the greatest gift: God Himself, God as our faithful Father in Christ Jesus, through the constant presence of the Holy Spirit. When we know God, we slowly learn to reappraise what is truly valuable:

> Before, the soul sought after this and that, but now it says, "I see that it is not necessary for me to be rich, but it is necessary for me to make my peace with God; it is not necessary that I should live a pleasurable life in this world, but it is absolutely necessary that I should have pardon of my sin; it is not necessary that I should have honour and preferment, but it is necessary that I should have God as my portion, and have my part in Jesus Christ, and it is necessary that my soul should be saved in the day of Jesus Christ."[14]

When we have God as our portion, much that is not truly necessary in our life can begin to fade from view. In Christ, we have what is necessary.

This is how God's people have always been able to remain unwavering in praise. For instance, the prophet Habakkuk resolves to trust in God, no matter what happens to the land and people and temple. Even when the Babylonians invade and all the fields are ruined and the flocks are no more, Habakkuk will thank the Lord:

13. Lewis, *Letters to Malcolm*, 93.
14. Burroughs, *Rare Jewel*, 92.

Though the fig tree may not blossom,
Nor fruit be on the vines;
Though the labor of the olive may fail,
And the fields yield no food;
Though the flock may be cut off from the fold,
And there be no herd in the stalls—
Yet I will rejoice in the LORD,
I will joy in the God of my salvation. (Hab. 3:17–18)

God teaches us to rejoice in Him as the sovereign Lord, the One who does only what is right, the One who never missteps. Though the disease is spreading and the brokenness can't be fixed, though there is no money in the account and the loved one is in the grave, we can still be thankful. Even then, "I will rejoice in the LORD, I will joy in the God of my salvation" (Hab. 3:18). We rejoice because we believe that this God is with us, and He is for us. We give thanks because we believe that He is our God in Christ and that in Him we will live forever.

Thanking God for the Thorn

Like many believers, the apostle Paul was well acquainted with suffering. In 2 Corinthians 12:7 he describes one of his hardships as "a thorn in the flesh." For years Paul was troubled by something, the exact nature of which is unknown to us: possibly a mental burden, a physical handicap, or the suffering that accompanied his ministry. Paul pleaded with the Lord three times to remove it. And from a human perspective, surely Paul could have accomplished more for the Lord if he was freed from this trial.

But God gave a simple answer to Paul's anguished pleading about his thorn: "My grace is sufficient for you, for My strength is made perfect in weakness" (2 Cor. 12:9). Christ wanted Paul to rest in His grace alone, more valuable than any notion of human strength, wisdom, or health. It is because of this grace that Paul can affirm that he is content (Phil. 4:11–13). Because of this same grace, every child of God can echo Paul's words. Through adversity we learn to rest in the all-sufficiency of our Lord and Savior.

And when our suffering leads us to treasure God's grace, perhaps we can come to the point where we thank God for the thorn. Such was the testimony of George Matheson. He was a Scottish minister and hymn writer from the nineteenth century, perhaps most well known for the hymn "O Love That Wilt Not Let Me Go." Matheson began to lose his eyesight in his youth, and he was completely blind by age twenty. Because of Matheson's physical handicap, his fiancée ended their engagement, and he was plunged into despair. But by God's grace, his sufferings did not render him unfruitful. Matheson served the church capably for many years, and he gave expression to his faith through songs and other writings. In a sermon he once reflected on the blessing of his thorn:

> My God, I have never thanked Thee for my thorn. I have thanked Thee a thousand times for my roses, but never once for my thorn. I have been looking forward to a world where I shall get compensation for my cross, but I have never thought of my cross as itself a present glory.... Teach me the glory of my cross, teach me the value of my thorn. Show me that I have climbed to Thee the path of pain.[15]

For those in the middle of terrible pain or hurt, it can sound callous to thank God for the thorn. Right now, the prospect of unrelieved suffering might be incredibly hard. Gratitude might seem almost inappropriate.

But in distress, a child of God returns to the promises of Scripture. There we see that the Father's loving discipline always bears good fruits (Heb. 12:5–7). And there we see Paul's confidence in Romans 8:18: "I consider that the sufferings of this present time are not worthy to be compared to the glory which shall be revealed." In all our suffering we have hope—an unseen hope but true, a firm

---

15. George Matheson, "Thanks for the Thorn," in *Moments on the Mount: A Series of Devotional Meditations* (London: James Nisbet, 1884), 61–62, https://www.google.com/books/edition/Moments_on_the_Mount/WcwCAAAAQAAJ?hl=en&gbpv=1.

hope that will not disappoint. In Christ we have a hope to hold on to
and to thank God for in all circumstances.

Reflect ...

◆ When have you found it hard to thank the Lord? Why?

◆ How can you thank God in all circumstances?

◆ If God has brought suffering into your life, how has He helped
you to remain grateful?

◆ What are some of the thorns in your life? Have you been able to
thank God for the thorn?

CHAPTER 9

Forever Thanksgiving

Gratitude lies just beneath the surface throughout the grand story of Scripture. We see hints of this theme at every pivotal moment in God's redemptive plan. God created humankind to render thanksgiving to Him. Having bestowed every good gift on our first parents, God expected their devoted obedience forever. But despite God's generosity, Adam and Eve did not glorify Him. They rejected the Giver and corrupted His good gifts—in short, they were ungrateful (Rom. 1:21). Even so, God did not consign us to the misery of thanklessness and its penalty. In Christ He forgives our ingratitude and every associated sin, and He begins to instill in us the virtue of thanksgiving by Christ's Spirit.

The theme of thankfulness thus links Scripture's key theme of creation, fall, and redemption. And so we aren't surprised to detect this theme in the very last chapter of God's plan: restoration.

Getting Ready

God created us for thanksgiving. And when Christ returns, He will perfectly restore this spirit and activity in His people. As we journey onward to the perfection of worshipful gratitude, we still have much to learn. Recall the many ways in which the spirit and practice of gratitude are undermined in our life:

- We forget to thank God.
- We turn His gifts into idols.

- We act as if we are entitled to His blessings.
- We take His gifts for granted.
- We become discontent.
- We claim the credit for good things received.

Much inhibits our thankful response to the God of all grace, but we are grateful that He isn't done with us yet. He is busy changing us in a glorious process of transformation (2 Cor. 3:18). God is shaping us into "the image of His Son" (Rom. 8:29), renewing us until we become like Christ, the only man who lived in flawless thanksgiving to God.

Already today we are preparing for the eternal project of gratitude. We look forward to an intensification of our reasons for gratitude when God grants eternal blessing in Christ. In the peace of eternity, we will not only enjoy the ability to express our thanksgiving to God flawlessly, but we will also delight in the rich increase of His gifts. Such is the glorious prospect that Jesus promises His believers.

Until He Comes

In an earlier chapter, we saw the Lord's Supper as the ultimate thanksgiving feast. Jesus gave bread and wine so that our faith can be frequently nourished by His sacrifice on the cross. Thanksgiving is the joyous atmosphere at the Lord's Table because the heart of this meal is the covenant fellowship we may enjoy with God through Christ.

While the Lord's Supper looks back on the finished work of Jesus, the sacrament also looks forward to how He will consummate God's saving plan. Jesus's own words at the supper indicate this expectation: "I will not drink of this fruit of the vine from now on until that day when I drink it new with you in My Father's kingdom" (Matt. 26:29). Pao explains, "Jesus himself points to the messianic banquet when the power of the cross will be fully realized."[1] After the cross comes glory; after the darkness of Godforsakenness, there is a brighter day. Jesus knows His death will not be a final disappointing

---

1. Pao, *Thanksgiving: An Investigation of a Pauline Theme*, 131.

chapter, but just the beginning. God will use it as the cornerstone for His kingdom.

We look ahead with anticipation to when Christ will drink the wine "new" with us. It will be new, not discolored by the old order of things, contaminated by sin, but restored—like *all* creation will be restored. From that great day and ever onward, we will enjoy perfect fellowship with Christ our Savior. Then the bread and the wine will no longer be signs and seals, standing for things unseen. In fact, there will be no need for sacraments, for the Savior Himself will be in our midst. This is why Paul says, "For as often as you eat this bread and drink this cup, you proclaim the Lord's death till He comes" (1 Cor. 11:26). Christ died, He rose, He is coming again, and He invites us to a wedding feast that we get to enjoy forever.

One day soon, our celebration of salvation will become so much better. The next time that He drinks a cup of wine, it will be with us! When He returns, we will eat a feast for celebration. It will be an everlasting wedding banquet held in honor of the Son and His beautiful bride. "To remember Jesus' death and to offer thanks for this climactic act of history is, therefore, to look forward to his return."[2] Every time we participate in Christ's sacrament, we are pointed ahead to future thanksgiving, full and perfect.

Future Thanksgiving

Thanksgiving often arises from a meditation on the past works of the Lord. When we remember God's great saving deeds in the past, and when we recollect how He answered our prayers in times of crisis, our spirit of thanksgiving revives. Remembering, we are compelled to offer fresh words of praise.

But Christian thanksgiving does more than look back. Once again, it is not only retrospective, but prospective. Because we know the unchanging God, the Lord whose "mercy endures forever" (Ps. 136:1), we can also look ahead with gratitude. We fully expect a wealth of future blessings. God's mercies are new every morning

---

2. Pao, *Thanksgiving: An Investigation of a Pauline Theme*, 131.

(Lam. 3:22–23), and they will be, even on the final morning of this present earth!

As he does with so many aspects of gratitude, Paul models this future thanksgiving. In 1 Corinthians 15, he addresses the essential reality of Christ's resurrection, the sure nature of the believer's hope, and the marvelous characteristics of the resurrected body. Building his teaching to a climax toward the end of the chapter, Paul speaks of how sin and death are swallowed up in Christ's triumph over the grave. And then he offers this thanksgiving: "But thanks be to God, who gives us the victory through our Lord Jesus Christ" (v. 57). Notice how Paul's thanksgiving is for a gift that has been granted in principle, but not in fullness. It is gratitude for grace that is already, but not yet. We thank God for our final victory because we're full of confidence that we will receive this gift.

The writer to the Hebrews exhorts us in a similar way. He looks ahead to our entrance into the presence of the holy God, together with the innumerable angels, the assembly of all believers, and Jesus as the Mediator of the new covenant. And he urges, "Therefore let us be grateful for receiving a kingdom that cannot be shaken, and thus let us offer to God acceptable worship, with reverence and awe" (Heb. 12:28 ESV). Be grateful today for tomorrow's unshakable kingdom. Thank God for what He promised that you will receive!

For what good gifts do you expect to be thanking God forever? As you meditate on the promised glories of eternity, for what can you offer thanks to God today?

The Unending Anthem

Thanksgiving is prominent in Revelation, a part of Scripture that powerfully portrays God's work of restoration. Through John's visions, we are allowed a glimpse into heaven. Among the many spectacular sights in this divine panorama, we see that being in God's glorious presence inspires thanksgiving to Him. For instance, the twenty-four elders who sit before God on their thrones worship Him, saying, "*We give You thanks*, O Lord God Almighty, the One

who is and who was and who is to come" (Rev. 11:17). Thanksgiving
to God is the only fitting response.

We see this likewise in Revelation 7:12. There, the myriad angels
around God's throne, together with the elders and four living creatures, join in this chorus of praise:

> Amen! Blessing and glory and wisdom,
> *Thanksgiving* and honor and power and might,
> Be to our God forever and ever.

The highest possible adoration is to be given to God! It is surely not
accidental that there are *seven* qualities, a full number of God's perfections. In view of all that the triune God is, all that He has done,
and all that He will yet do, this heavenly choir sings that God is
worthy—worthy to receive thankful praise, worthy to possess glory
forever.

We can focus on just one of the seven elements ascribed to
God: *thanksgiving*. In the worshipers' words, "Thanksgiving...be to
our God, forever and ever." In verse 12, what is the reason for this
thanksgiving? Think of everything John has witnessed in Revelation.
He has beheld the unfolding of God's great plan for the world and
the church. For instance, in chapter 5, the Lamb is found worthy
to take the scroll and break its seals, fulfilling God's purposes for
redemption and judgment. The Lamb has been slain, yet the Lamb
lives, and all who belong to Him will also live. Says one of the elders
to John, "They shall neither hunger anymore nor thirst anymore; the
sun shall not strike them, nor any heat.... And God will wipe away
every tear from their eyes" (7:16–17).

In Christ, condemned prisoners like us are rescued from all our
deserved terrors and miseries. In Christ, filthy sinners are cleansed.
In Christ, we are allowed to approach God and remain with Him
in a recreated world. From beginning to end, this salvation is the
great work of God and the Lamb. Therefore, those who are standing
before the Lord lift up a song of worship: "Thanksgiving...be to our
God forever and ever" (7:12). The marvelous deeds of God inspire
an outpouring of thanks. The splendid triumph of Christ moves us

to celebrate the Lord. Thus, it has been rightly said, "Gratitude is the unending anthem of heaven."[3]

And so it should be for all the redeemed. We are not in heaven yet, but by faith we're part of the great multitude that no one can number. We are not yet wearing white robes, but by faith we share already in the perfect cleansing through Christ's blood. We can thank Him today and will thank Him forever.

Thank God Forever

The infinitely good and gracious God is worthy of infinite gratitude. E. M. Bounds writes about this future activity, "Praise and thanksgiving will be our blessed employment while we remain in heaven. Nor will we ever grow weary of this pleasing task."[4] We look forward to when our gratitude will be unending and unerring.

As we enjoy the presence of God in the recreated heavens and earth, our thanksgiving will surely be deepened by a remembrance of the Lord's great goodness. People sometimes conceive of heaven as a place without memory. And to an extent, one can understand this. If in heaven we remember the shameful record of our past sins, we might be sorrowful. Or if we think of loved ones who are absent from heaven's bliss, we might be filled with regret. But Revelation tells us that in His presence, "God will wipe away every tear," and there will be "[no] sorrow, nor crying" (21:4). So is every cause for sadness going to be stricken from our minds? Is heaven a place of eternal forgetfulness?

In previous chapters we've seen how the remembrance of God's mercies is a powerful prompt for gratitude. There is no reason to think that this will be any different in the next life. Heaven is not a place of eternal forgetfulness. Instead, we'll be filled with thanksgiving as we remember our sins and how they have been blotted out in Christ. We'll be grateful for the demonstration of God's justice against those who have not believed and His mercy for those joined

3. DeMoss, *Choosing Gratitude*, 75.
4. Bounds, "Essentials of Prayer," 310.

by faith to Jesus. We'll thank God that at last we can see clearly how He turned to our good all the sufferings of life. The thanksgiving refrain in Scripture reminds us of this unfailing mercy of God—a mercy that prevails everlastingly: "Oh, give thanks to the LORD, for He is good! For His mercy endures *forever*" (Ps. 106:1).

In Psalm 30, David sings joyously at the dedication of the tabernacle. Earthly worship is always flawed, so at the conclusion of the psalm, David anticipates the day of perfect worship, "to the end that my glory may sing praise to You and not be silent. O LORD my God, *I will give thanks to You forever*" (v. 12). He envisions a forever thanksgiving, when we will ceaselessly and tirelessly bring glory to God, who is worthy to be praised forever. On a similar theme, Joseph Addison wrote a hymn titled "When All Thy Mercies," pondering how the gratitude of the redeemed will fill eternity:

> Through all eternity to Thee
> A grateful song I'll raise;
> But, oh! Eternity's too short
> To utter all Thy praise.[5]

While we are in the middle of our sanctification, the project of becoming more grateful will never be completed. Not only is the inventory of our blessing never finished, but we still struggle against the ungrateful tendencies of our heart.

So we hope for that day when we'll be able to present perfect thanksgiving to God: no good gift forgotten, no blessing taken for granted, no credit claimed for benefits received, no sense of entitlement, no creaturely idols crafted, no spirit of discontentment—but all glory given to the triune God alone. It is when we finally enter His glorious presence that we will realize how much we owe.

Robert Murray M'Cheyne was a noted Scottish preacher and gifted poet who lived in the 1800s. Although he often suffered serious illness, he devoted his life to the work of preaching and mission. After contracting typhus fever, he went to the presence of his

---

5. Joseph Addison, "When All Thy Mercies," in the public domain.

Savior at age thirty. One of his poems, "I Am Debtor," explores the theme of a believer's indebtedness to God and how it would not be fully understood until he stood in Christ's presence. Here is a short excerpt from M'Cheyne's poem:

> When this passing world is done,
> When has sunk yon glaring sun,
> When we stand with Christ in glory,
> Looking o'er life's finished story,
> Then, Lord, shall I fully know—
> Not till then—how much I owe.
>
> When I hear the wicked call,
> On the rocks and hills to fall,
> When I see them start and shrink
> On the fiery deluge brink,
> Then, Lord, shall I fully know—
> Not till then—how much I owe.
>
> . . . .
>
> When I stand before the throne,
> Dressed in beauty not my own,
> When I see Thee as Thou art,
> Love Thee with unsinning heart,
> Then Lord, shall I fully know—
> Not till then—how much I owe.
>
> . . . .
>
> Chosen not for good in me,
> Wakened up from wrath to flee,
> Hidden in the Saviour's side,
> By the Spirit sanctified,
> Teach me, Lord, on earth to show,
> By my love, how much I owe.[6]

---

6. Andrew A. Bonar, *Memoir and Remains of Robert Murray M'Cheyne* (Edinburgh: Banner of Truth, 1966), 636–37.

Today's gratitude to God is only a small beginning of our eternal project. So we seek to grow in thankfulness. While we have life, we should tune our hearts for this forever song: "Thanksgiving be to our God, forever and ever." Begin today and continue always: "Give thanks to the Lord, for He is good." For when you have fought the good fight and finished the race, you'll still be thanking the God of all grace—forever and ever.

Reflect . . .

◆ How does the Lord's Supper instill in you a sense of future joy?

◆ For what good gifts do you expect to be thanking God forever?

◆ As you meditate on the promised glories of eternity, for what can you offer thanks to God today?

◆ Why is eternity too short to utter all God's praise?

Scripture Index

| 17:17 | 81 |
| 24:44 | 116 |

John
1:14	23
1:16	23–24
11:41	66–67
16:33	102, 109
21:25	2

Acts
17:24–25	72–73
17:25	30
17:27	30
17:31	30

Romans
1	14
1:8	101n12
1:21	14, 29, 83, 125
1:25	29, 83
1:32	29
3:23	38
5:1	118
5:3	117, 118
5:4	118, 119
6:23	39
8:18	123
8:29	126
8:32	34–35
8:38–39	102
8:39	55
10:9	39
10:15	58
11:35	64, 72, 80
12:1	39

1 Corinthians
1:4	101n12
4:7	3–4, 61, 89, 107, 117
10:16	36, 37
10:31	51

11:25	37
11:26	127
15:10	23
15:57	128

2 Corinthians
1:20	36
2:9	58
3:18	126
4:15	95
4:18	119
8–9	70
9:8	70–71
9:15	30, 63
12:7	122
12:9	122

Galatians
| 6:9 | 22 |
| 6:10 | 22 |

Ephesians
1:6	58
1:11	116
1:15–16	101
2:8	22
3:18–19	35
3:19	53
4:24	21
5	76
5:4	76–77
5:19–20	69
5:20	5, 9n6, 64

Philippians
1:3	101n12
1:29	57
4:6	9n6, 66
4:10–19	74
4:11–13	90, 122
4:19	26